REPAIR

REPAIR

The Impulse to Restore in a Fragile World

ELIZABETH V. SPELMAN

Beacon Press

BOSTON

Beacon Press
25 Beacon Street
Boston, Massachusetts 02108-2892
www.beacon.org

Beacon Press books
are published under the auspices of
the Unitarian Universalist Association of Congregations.

Printed in the United States of America

06 05 04 03 02 8 7 6 5 4 3 2 1

This book is printed on acid-free paper that meets the uncoated paper
ANSI/NISO specifications for permanence as revised in 1992.

Composition by Wilsted & Taylor Publishing Services

Library of Congress Cataloging-in-Publication Data
Spelman, Elizabeth V.
    Repair : the impulse to restore in a fragile world / Elizabeth V.
Spelman.
        p.   cm.
Includes bibliographical references and index.
    ISBN 0-8070-2012-5 (alk. paper)
    1. Psychology, Applied. 2. Repairing—Psychological aspects.
I. Title.
    BF636.S689 2002
    128'—dc21

                                              2002006175

IN MEMORY OF POP,
MY FAVORITE TINKERER

CONTENTS

CHAPTER I

Introducing *Homo reparans*

The Human Being is a repairing animal. Repair is ubiquitous, something we engage in every day and in almost every dimension of our lives. *Homo sapiens* is also *Homo reparans*.

Perhaps the most obvious kinds of repair are those having to do with the inanimate objects with which we surround ourselves—the clothes calling out for mending, the automobiles for fixing, the buildings for renovating, the works of art for restoring. But our bodies and souls also are by their very nature subject to fracture and fissure, for which we seek homely household recipes for healing and consolation, or perhaps the expert ministrations of surgeons, therapists, and other menders and fixers of all manner of human woes. Relationships between individuals and among nations are notoriously subject to fraying and being rent asunder. From apologies and other informal attempts at patching things up to law courts, conflict mediation, and truth and reconciliation commissions, we try to reweave what we revealingly call the social fabric. No wonder, then, that *H. reparans* is always and everywhere on call: we, the world we live in, and the objects and relationships we create are by their very nature things that can break, decay, unravel, fall to pieces.

Our reparative repertoire is vast, something readily and richly attested to by sources ranging from *Reader's Digest* stories about legendary handymen[1] to essays in professional philosophy journals on the ethics of environmental restoration;[2] from Dave Barry's send-ups of men's delusions about their superior repairing skills[3] to legal treatises weighing monetary reparations against the work of truth and reconciliation commissions;[4] from *The You Don't Need a Man to Fix It Book: The Woman's Guide to Confident Home Repair*[5] to *Tikkun,* the journal emblazoned with the Hebrew phrase *tikkun olam,* to repair the world. Newspapers and magazines provide a steady stream of reports on the vast variety of projects and problems awaiting *H. reparans:* former President Bill Clinton has "a reputation to salvage," though he and former Vice President Al Gore are said to have "patched up their tattered relationship."[6] Citizens in Cincinnati, Ohio, are working on "repairing civic morale" in response to heightened racial tensions.[7] A team of conservators at the Stedelijk Museum in Amsterdam has successfully met "one of the biggest challenges of their profession: how to repair, seamlessly, a large-format, basically monochromatic canvas" (Barnett Newman's *Cathedra*).[8] *Consumer Reports* regularly offers advice on whether to "Fix it or nix it," "Fix it or sell it."[9] The wide range of responses to the horrible wounds inflicted on September

11, 2001, bear solemn witness to the sheer variety of *H. reparans'* capacities: The twin towers can neither be repaired nor restored, but as the president of the Historic Districts Council of New York City sees it, whatever is done at the site "must reweave the damaged threads of fabric that terrorism sought to tear apart, and create a sense of place that fills the void and honors the losses of Sept. 11."[10] In one issue alone of the *New York Times Magazine,* there were stories devoted to the tasks of "mending a psyche" and of figuring out "how to put the family back together."[11] An op-ed essay by former Secretary of the Treasury Robert Rubin on September 30 described "A Post-Disaster Economy in Need of Repair."[12]

H. reparans also can be found wondering whether sometimes it isn't the better part of wisdom to leave the flaws, the fragments, the ruins, alone: Restorers of *Gone With the Wind* had to decide whether a flaw in the original should "be fixed or retained as an intrinsic part of the original masterpiece";[13] echoing the fate of Humpty-Dumpty, a political columnist counsels her readers, "You don't have to be abused or betrayed to have a bad marriage—a marriage that cannot be fixed, even with the help of all the therapists on the Upper West Side, or all the preachers in Louisiana."[14] A sticker on the bottom of a painted floor mat instructs users, "Over time, you may notice slight yellowing or cracking. These imperfections are consistent with the nature of hand-made mats and are NOT considered flaws, but rather a normal part of the life and character of these mats."[15]

The English language is generously stocked with words

for the many preoccupations and occupations of *H. re-parans:* repair, restore, rehabilitate, renovate, reconcile, redeem, heal, fix, and mend—and that's the short list. Such linguistic variety is not gratuitous. These are distinctions that make a difference. Do you want the car repaired, so that you can continue to commute to work? Or do you want it restored, so that you can display it in its original glory? Is a patch on that jacket adequate, or do you insist on invisible mending, on having it look as if there never were a rip to begin with? Should that work of art be restored, or simply preserved? Why do some ecologists want to preserve an environment rather than try to repair the damage done to it? Does forgiveness necessarily restore a ruptured relationship or simply allow a resumption of it? What does an apology achieve that monetary reparations cannot—and vice versa? What was thought to be at stake for citizens of the new South Africa in the contrast between restorative justice and retributive justice—between the healing promised by a Truth and Reconciliation Commission and the punishment exacted through an adversarial court system?

As crucial as such distinctions are, the family of repair activities shares the aim of maintaining some kind of continuity with the past in the face of breaks or ruptures to that continuity. They involve returning in some manner or other to an earlier state—to the bowl before it was broken, to the friendship before it began to buckle under the weight of suspicion, to the nation before it was torn apart by hostility and war. Even though taking superglue to the bowl repairs it without fully restoring it to its preshattered condition, both repairer and restorer want to pick up a thread with the past. Their work appears to involve something distinctly different from the original creation of the bowl, but also from its accidental or deliberate destruction, its abandonment, or the serendipitous retrieval of its shards for flowerpot filler. In a similar fashion, there is a difference between putting a friendship back together and simply letting it hobble on, decisively ending it, or making a new friend altogether.

In short, as varied as the activities of *H. reparans* are, they appear to be notably different from other kinds of relations to or attitudes toward the past. Creators start anew, they do not repair what already exists (though we shall find reason to question too neat a distinction between creating and repairing); destroyers want to get rid of what's there, not rescue it; noninterferers neither help nor hinder, simply allowing things to degenerate or decay; replacers figure it's not possible or worth it to repair; *bricoleurs* collect and make use of pieces of the past but do not try to return them to an earlier function.

Repair wouldn't be necessary if things never broke, never frayed, never splintered or fell to pieces—or if we didn't care that they did. A world in which repair was not necessary would either be filled with unchanging unbreakable eternal objects (a version, perhaps, of Plato's world of Forms) or a junk heap, things, people, and relationships abandoned when they no longer functioned in the requisite manner. To repair is to acknowledge and respond to the fracturability of the world in which we live in a very particular way—not by simply throwing our hands up in despair at the damage, or otherwise accepting without question that there is no possibility of or point in trying to put the pieces back together, but by employing skills of mind, hand, and heart to recapture an earlier moment in the history of an object or a relationship in order to allow it to keep existing.

H. reparans has been known to take great satisfaction in exercising the capacity to repair, and pride in what the result of such exercise can do for broken-down cars, torn retinas, and frayed partnerships. Indeed, sometimes we take greater pleasure in having a well-repaired object than an unbroken one, prefer (if we're lucky enough to have options) living in a neighborhood of renovated houses to one in which the buildings are all spanking new, enjoy a friendship that has known apology and forgiveness more than one protected from the risks of being rent. We seem at least sometimes to welcome the sentiment that things are stronger in the broken places.

At the same time, a voracious appetite for fixing can lead to poor judgment about what is and is not desirable or even possible to repair. Pride in our repairing abilities may push us into believing that whatever has been broken can be and ought to be fixed. Recognition of occasions on which such a belief is wrongheaded can provide, on the one hand, comic relief: "I was able, thanks to my experience as a homeowner and my natural mechanical sense, to get pieces of insulation deep into my nose."[16] On the other hand, tragic grief over irreparable loss—for example, the death of a child—reminds us of how much there is that cannot be undone, how thoroughly inappropriate the confidence that there is nothing that can't be fixed. Indeed, some scholars of Holocaust survivor testimonies insist that we seriously misread those accounts if we take their point to be some kind of healing or repair: "All attempts to investigate the effects of atrocity on a group or a community must begin with the narratives of individual victims . . . which mock the very idea that traumas can be healed."[17] We do not always mourn what we cannot repair. Sometimes the irreparable has been the source of complex delights, as we might learn from the reflections of Rose Macaulay and others on the pleasure in historical ruins[18] or fascination with what, in the full title of a recent book, is called *Demolition: The Art of Demolishing, Dismantling, Imploding, Toppling and Razing*[19]—though leisurely delight at planned demolition seems particularly luxurious against scenes of horrific destruction such as those witnessed on September 11.

We live at a time—though perhaps this has always been true—in which there is on the one hand worry that our capacities for repair are atrophying as we become habituated to throwing out broken things and moving from one imperfect relationship to the next, and on the other hand concern that we are so enamored of our reparative talents that we intervene where we should not. So, we are told that "Americans, infantilized by labor-saving devices and a service industry that has put even the smallest mending or cleaning task into the hands of professionals, no longer feel at home in their own homes";[20] but also that we live in "a culture sustained by the faith that there are technical fixes for all human ills."[21]

What, then, is to be gained from an exploration of the projects and habitats of *H. reparans,* from watching all that fixing and mending, from observing how much of the life of *Homo sapiens* involves judging what it is possible and desirable to repair? Such judgments disclose in an intimate way what we do and do not value about ourselves and the people and things around us. For though we do not repair everything we value, we would not repair things unless they were in some sense valuable to us, and how they matter to us shows up in the form of repair we undertake: Repairing a broken chair in order to make it serviceable is different from restoring it in order to exhibit its original beauty or display the owner's wealth or good taste. Our coming to grips with the reparable and the irreparable also is the scene of comedy—of our bumbling attempts to undo damage—and of tragedy—of stark and hard-earned realization that the damage cannot be undone. Reflection on the ubiquity and variety of the activities engaged in by *H. reparans* brings into bright relief some prominent features of the world we inhabit—its mutability and impermanence—and a range of skills we deploy in response to that world.

CHAPTER 2

From Bricolage
to Invisible Mending

If there is a quintessential repairperson, it is Willie, the crackerjack mechanic in rural upstate New York carefully and lovingly described in Douglas Harper's *Working Knowledge: Skill and Community in a Small Shop.*[1] Willie— we never learn his last name—specializes in Saab automobiles, but he also works on tractors, furnaces, and other equipment necessary for life in a remote and seasonally snowbound part of the United States. Willie's customers do not have very deep pockets, and they count on him to keep resurrecting machinery that better-heeled farmers and teachers would long ago have consigned to the junk heap.

People come to Willie for repairs, not for new cars, not to have their old ones restored to mint condition. His job is to make sure that once again the engine runs, the wheels move, the doors and windows open and close, the roof doesn't leak. Though he might in the meantime do some basic maintenance—replace the oil or tighten a belt—his central aim is to get the car back into running order, back into a condition worth maintaining.

In Willie's shop there is very little routine repair: standard responses to standard failures or damages are not the order of the day. As Willie sees it, part of the challenge of the work is that "no job's the same"; there are contingencies and anomalies that can't be anticipated by computer programs or instruction manuals. " 'If you had a thousand jobs in a year, not two of those thousand would be the same. Even the ones that are supposed to be the same aren't. Things are broken or worn in different ways—they each have their own characteristics' " (169).

Though diagnostic equipment is available on the market, Willie is not inclined to depend upon it, relying instead on a deep acquaintance with the materials he works with, calling on knowledge not only of how something is supposed to function but of how things feel: " '[I]t's just like your fingers got eyes. If you've got a nut, or a stud, someplace and you want to know what size it is and you couldn't see it, you've got to be able to reach in, feel it, and tell.' "[2] From head to toe, Willie is alive to the sources of information in the objects in his hands and at the far end of his tools.

Douglas Harper's portrait of Willie, animated by an unspoken desire to make sure we fully appreciate the rich mix of Willie's skills, implicitly responds to a widespread ambivalence about repair work: On the one hand, we treat such work as mundane and humble, something anyone can do, a good alternative to brainier and more complex kinds of challenges (hence, for example, the separation of vocational schools from ordinary high schools); on the other hand, we often act as if people who, like Willie, do such fantastic repair jobs are so few and far between that they ought to be thought of as local heroes/heroines, that they should be treated as national treasures. And indeed Tom and Ray Magliozzi, brother co-hosts of the radio call-in show, *Car Talk,* enjoy wide popularity and admiration for their diagnostic skills, which seem only partly explained by their MIT educations.

Still, repairers as a group do not seem to be held in the kind of esteem that, for example, inventors and their inventions are; there is not a Repairer's Hall of Fame analogous to the Lemelson Center for the Study of Invention and Innovation at the Smithsonian Institution in Washington, D.C. Repair work such as Willie's, at least on the face of it, is far too derivative: As a repairer of objects created by other people, he has, as he says, to put himself " 'in the place of the engineer who built [them] in the first place' " (127). He has to understand how someone else designed the car to function in order to get it functioning again. Moreover, unlike an automobile manufacturer or dealer, Willie does not have a made-to-order parts shop. What he does have is a huge supply of pieces and parts, odds and ends whose original purpose in life may long have been forgotten. His inventory has been put together from the scraps left over from his own and other people's projects, most of which have nothing to do with whatever his current project is. Willie is, in short, a *bricoleur,* someone who makes do with what is at hand by envisioning new uses for remnants and leftovers. As a repairer, then,

Willie's work derives from and thus is circumscribed by the creative designs of others; as a *bricoleur*, he is constrained by the contingency of what happens to be at hand.

However, in someone with Willie's skills and patience, such constraints become opportunities for ingenious design. Harper remarks that much of the work Willie does would not be possible if he were "locked into established ways of seeing or doing" (6), if he were bound tightly to the original design or unable to imagine a use for what other people call "junk" to solve a current problem. In the process of repairing a piece of machinery Willie often, in fact, redesigns a part—a door handle, for example—correcting flaws in the original design rather than trying to adhere to it: "Willie's knowledge of materials helps him understand *why* machines have deteriorated or broken down, and it leads him to see the act of repair as remedying an engineering flaw rather than replacing a part" (73). In an economic context in which making do is often the only option for Willie and his customers, Willie is able to "redefine the fixability of objects" (34). When irreparability is not an option, or in any event the judgment of irreparability is put off as long as possible, Willie's deep understanding of what he is working with, his knowing how to communicate with rather than fight his materials, and his willingness and ability not to be bound by preexisting design and the original uses of old parts allow him to do the work that has become indispensable to his small community.

★   ★   ★

Then there is Fred Haefele, lovesick over a dilapidated Indian Chief motorcycle he espies beneath the superannuated cookware, musical instruments, sporting equipment, and other discarded denizens of an overstuffed garage:

> There it is—that thing I've been looking for all along: a mottled steel frame, crouching in the midst of all this debris, an engineless skeleton on a pair of rubberless rims. A gearshift lever and disarticulated clutch pedal dangle from the frame, and a pair of rusty gas tanks are fixed loosely in place. Those areas of the tanks not dinged up or peppered with the holes of abortive bodywork are painted a kind of mustard-phlegm color.[3]

Fred is burning not simply to repair the vintage machine but to restore it, make it resemble as closely as possible such a vehicle in its original state. Since he understands a restored motorcycle to be by definition not an original (63)—if the original isn't already for all intents and purposes extinct, the very act of restoration completes its erasure—Fred thinks of his restoration job not as bringing back the original machine but as rebuilding a "basketcase."

So, given the state of the bike, Fred is not in a position to keep it in its original condition. He hopes, however, to restore the bike, and in that sense turn the clock back. The more "authentic" the restoration, the more the bike will resemble an original machine as it came off the factory floor. Missing or irreparably damaged original parts are to be replaced if at all possible by authentic parts of the same vintage machine. A good portion of Fred's time is spent hunting down such parts and trying to confirm their provenance. Reproductions may be necessary, but they are lamentable, no matter how historically accurate: "Since there are no fenders included . . . I will probably have to buy reproductions, which means the tanks will be the only original sheet metal on the bike" (36).

Even safety-enhancing redesign of the placement of shift and throttle controls, which in their original formation produce "synaptic meltdown," is to be resisted: "I could have converted the controls—lots of restorers do. But in an effort to enter into the spirit of the thing, I opted for the authentic factory style" (189).

Indeed, the closer the bike comes to replicating an original, the more worried Fred becomes about actually *using* it: "I'm not riding this bike anywhere. I might put a scratch on it" (144). Fred doesn't act on the threat—his pleasure in riding the bike, and his contempt for restorers who bring their bikes to rallies on a truck bed, overpower his concerns about the inevitable damage the restored bike will have to endure—but he's painfully aware that his heroic efforts will begin to be compromised the minute the bike is put to ordinary use.

Fred is concerned as much about the authenticity of the restorative process as he is about the authenticity of the restored bike. For him there is all the difference in the world between scrounging around in old garages with one's buddies, trying to find the right parts, and running a tidy, fully supplied professional shop: It's the difference between "a craft that has long been the domain of the workingman, a labor of love that, for decades, took place in chilly garages all over the country" and a "high-end business" (50); between "a wild skunk works collective . . . involving the skills of a whole community of artisans, craftsmen, and friends, a project that had us all fixing, fabricating, and scavenging parts in a sweaty back-alley garage" and "sanitized top-dollar" outfits that pride themselves on tidier, more efficient, highly rationalized ways of going about restoration (201).

Louise Wijnberg greets me at the entrance to the Stedelijk Museum in Amsterdam, and we go immediately to a specially cordoned-off area of what normally is exhibition space to examine the back side of Barnett Newman's *Cathedra*. The huge canvas, lying facedown in what amounts to a made-to-order wooden operating table, was severely slashed with a Stanley knife in late 1997 (another Newman painting, *Who's Afraid of Red, Yellow and Blue III,* was the object of the same person's rage eleven years earlier).

Louise Wijnberg and her colleagues Elisabeth Bracht and Irene Glanzer are the painting conservators at the Stedelijk. Their first task was to stabilize the painting to prevent any further damage. Before the restoration work could begin, they had to find out what materials Newman himself had worked with and how he had applied them, double-checking along the way the accuracy of the museum's information about the painting. It also was crucial for them to know whether there had been any prior restorations and the nature of materials used in any such projects.[4]

Following current international restoration protocols, Louise, Elisabeth, and Irene had to make sure that anything they did could be reversed without damage to the work; they were to exercise the utmost restraint in either "filling in lacunae or removing materials and/or components" (29). At every stage of their work they were to be in consultation with specialists, including experts on restoration ethics, on monochrome paintings, on the Newman *oeuvre*.

Louise, Elisabeth, and Irene do in the art world what in the tailoring trades is called invisible mending: They try to fix the painting in such a way that it will look as if it never had been ripped. At the same time, their work is not supposed to be a secret: The distinction between the work of art and their surgical intervention must be kept clear. Careful records of what they have done must be kept so that if need be it can be undone. The more their work is necessary and present, the more the creation of the artist has disappeared. Hence the delicacy of their work in service to an art world in which "an artist's originality, style, development, and treatment of a subject" are central; our understanding of the artist and his work "would be seriously hampered if the distinction between his handiwork and that of his restorers could not be drawn."[5] Fred honors the designer of the motorcycle by replicating that design as closely as possible, but that involves his vastly transforming the machine he actually starts with. Louise, Elisabeth, and Irene honor the creator of the work of art by keeping their own handiwork to a minimum, neither editing nor revising, and surely not replicating from the ground up.

Because the restorers work in a context in which maintaining the distinction between the artist and the restorers is so important, they won't be called in unless absolutely necessary. Not all damage invites attention: As Catherine Elgin has put it, "some damage is too minor to matter; some too extensive to repair" (105)—too extensive in the sense that either the damage is irreparable or while, technically speaking, repair is possible, it would change the work beyond recognition or radically alter its value. In this case, restorers probably wouldn't have been called in if the vandal had slashed the canvas to shreds.

In the cultural context in which Louise and her colleagues work, the value of a work of art depends on its being an original, something directly created by the hand of the artist. A change in the state of that original can—but need not—detract from the value of the work; it may even enhance it. For example, patina might be welcomed for a variety of reasons, including its capacity to bring attention to aspects of a work of art that might otherwise escape our notice.[6] The very fact that patina is not only allowed but welcomed tells us, Elgin says, that the aim of restoration of works of art is not "the removal of the effects of time" but "the reversal of the ravages of time" (105): A change in the condition of the work of art does not necessarily constitute damage, and restorers who don't know the meaning of the distinction between damaging and nondamaging change may end up destroying the value of the objects under their care in the very process of trying to fix them. What constitutes damage is highly context-dependent: After all, the very same people who find any signs of aging in their own bodies abhorrent might welcome just the "right" signs of age in the houses they inhabit or the artworks they cherish.

★   ★   ★

Willie, Fred Haefele, Louise Wijnberg, Elisabeth Bracht, and Irene Glanzer: repairers all, readily identifiable embodiments of *Homo reparans* coming to grips with the plain and undeniable fact that the inanimate stuff *Homo sapiens* surrounds itself with is subject to breaking, fraying, decaying, disintegrating, degenerating, being damaged. Drawing on intimate knowledge of their materials and on enviable improvisatory skills, these repairers and restorers nurse cars and motorcycles and paintings back into a condition in which such objects can serve their appointed functions as safe moving vehicles, or exemplars of classic designs, or significant works of art. And yet we can't help but notice the difference in their aims and in the variety of constraints under which they labor.

Willie has completed his work when the car once again can perform its basic function of safely transporting people and their goods. It's immaterial for his purposes how the car looks or where the parts came from. His allegiance is to the road-worthiness of the car and the norms of mechanical efficiency. He's very interested in what the designer and manufacturer had in mind, how they intended the car and its parts to function, but if in the process of repairing the car he can make improvements, there is nothing to stop him; he is not in thrall to the original design or designer. In fact he often as not replaces door handles on certain Saabs with a redesigned version of his own that is much less likely than the original to malfunction.

Fred has bound himself not to take such liberties, in fact to do whatever he can to avoid them. His allegiance is to the authenticity of the restoration, to norms of historical accuracy and aesthetic appropriateness, which he regards as givens.[7] He does want the bike to run again, and to run perfectly, but the pleasure and pride he takes in the restored vehicle also make him reluctant to ride it or to depart from the original design, even if changes would enhance his safety. The more he knows about the original design, the better he can adhere to it. Because the point of the restoration is to celebrate and pay homage to the original, redesign is profane; reproduction parts, however historically accurate, are to be avoided as much as possible. Bricolage is out of the question: While Willie may spend a lot of his time rifling through old parts he's kept on hand just in case they might be useful for who knows what down the road, Fred spends a lot of his time hunting down original parts that he can use for their original intended purpose. The challenge for Willie's imagination is to devise new designs or new uses for old parts; the challenge for Fred's imagination is to find ways, against the odds, to adhere to the designs of others.

Louise Wijnberg, Elisabeth Bracht, and Irene Glanzer clearly cannot take the kind of liberties in their work that Willie does in his. They can't use just any old paint lying around or entertain thoughts of redesigning Newman's creation. And while like Fred they aim to adhere to specific criteria of historical and aesthetic accuracy, unlike Fred they cannot scrape off as much paint as they'd like, let alone rebuild the painting more or less from scratch. They are to do as little as possible to the object, strive as best they can to leave no visible evidence of their rescue work.

Though in one sense Fred's work is self-effacing—he tries to make it look as if the bike had never suffered any damage at all and thus as if his work had not been necessary—in another sense it clearly is not, since the pleasure and pride he takes in the restoration are in the very visible fruits of his handiwork: Everyone is supposed to know that this is a restoration and that it is Fred's. His bike in its own way is as much Indian-Chief-by-Fred as one of Willie's interesting hybrids is a Saab-by-Willie. But Louise, Elisabeth, and Irene are not supposed to make a Newman-by-Wijnberg-Bracht-and-Glanzer. Their handiwork is not supposed to be visible; their interpolations are to be kept to the absolute minimum.

Differences among Willie, Fred, and Louise/Elisabeth/Irene become particularly vivid if we imagine for a moment any of them deploying the tricks and obeying the formal and informal protocols of their trades in the shops of the others. If Willie were to work on Fred's motorcycle, following his ordinary protocols, he wouldn't be bothered about the authenticity of the parts nor be anxious about adhering to the original design. His labors would produce not that exact replica of a classic motorcycle of which Fred fervently dreams, but a veritable patchwork quilt of a bike, perhaps none of the parts matching but the whole put together in such a way that the machine runs smoothly and safely. Since Willie is not bound by the ethos of his own trade to restrain his creative impulses while fixing things, he might come up with a much sturdier repair to the slash in the Newman painting than the minimalist mending Elisabeth and her co-workers are obliged to produce.

Since it's perfectly allowable for him to leave visible evidence of his rescue work, Willie can change the appearance of the painting, thereby destroying its value as an original Newman.

Similarly, if Fred wandered into Willie's garage, with his own strict rules for rebuilding intact, he'd want to get every last Saab into the condition it was when it left the factory floor. He'd have to throw out all of Willie's *bricoleur* "junk" and stock up on "authentic" Saab parts. He'd be ready to tell customers that fumbling with ill-working door handles is the price of living with the real thing. Let loose in the Stedelijk, he'd certainly share Elisabeth and Irene and Louise's determination to find and use original paints. But committed as he is to the view that there is no damage that is good damage, no wear that enhances rather than detracts, he'd go about trying to get that Newman painting back into the condition it was when it left the artist's studio. And he'd bristle at the thought of "professionals" from the art world overseeing his work. He'd be beholden to his fellow rebuilders, not to stuffy museum directors or financiers worried about the monetary value of the work.

Louise and her colleagues wouldn't know where to begin in Willie's garage. After all, there is nothing there that is the work of an individual artist. If there were—perhaps there's an automobile that has the signature of a single artist, even of a small group of artists, rather than the insignia of a manufacturer—Louise and her co-conservators would find out as much as they could about the materials out of which the vehicle was made, the history of damage to it, and of earlier repairs or restorations. They would do their best not to leave any signs of their own work on the car, and they'd keep detailed records in the likely event that future restorers will want to undo their handiwork. When they put in a stop at Fred's shop, they'll once again wonder whether there could possibly be any work for them, in the absence of motorcycles bearing the signature of a single artist rather than a brand name. Actually what comes closest to that is Fred's own rebuilt bike. Indeed, given the way Fred himself treats the machine, he would no doubt prefer that art restorers approach his creation the way they do the Newman, rather than handle it the way he worked on the basketcase. When those inevitable dings and scratches damage his "work of art," he'd want it restored in the art restorative way—with respect for the artist who created it—not rebuilt in the Fred way—where any evidence of earlier handiwork is blasted or sanded or thrown away.

We know all this about Willie and Fred and Louise/ Elisabeth/Irene, which is why we don't take damaged works of art to Willie's shop, or go to Fred if our primary concern is to get the pickup back on the road in time to help a friend move to new lodgings. We know that the protocols Willie follows in his repair work would destroy Fred's rebuilding projects, ruin Elisabeth, Louise, and Irene's heroic restorations. We know there is not a single all-purpose repair shop, that the Willies and Freds and Irenes and Elisabeths and Louises of the world have the different work they do because we have devised a wide range of campaigns to confront the brute facts of the impermanence, imperfection, and fragility of the objects with which we cohabit the world. One approach is to embrace, even celebrate, such facts: Ruinists, for example—we'll be hearing more about them in a later chapter—rush to sites of decay and disrepair (Tintern Abbey, Angkor Wat, among others), reveling or at least finding instruction in the inevitability of the disintegration of the humanmade world. But Willie, Fred, Elisabeth, Louise, and Irene are hardly ruinists. They are, at least in their fields of expertise, devotees of repair. To choose from among the quite different modes of repair they offer is to choose a way of resisting or delaying the inexorable march of decay and disrepair. It is to toy with certain illusions and seek out certain consolations about the impermanence and inevitable decay of the objects around us.

Fred's rebuilt bike offers the illusion that time has not passed, that no change has taken place, that no damages have been incurred. Of course, we also see right through the illusion—if we couldn't, if we didn't or couldn't know the bike is not an original but a rebuilt, there would be nothing for Fred to feel proud of, nothing for us to admire. If time really could stand still, rebuilding the motorcycle wouldn't have been necessary. Perhaps what Fred offers is not so much the illusion that time has not passed as the consolation that time's passing isn't as bad as we might have thought, since with the requisite knowledge, skills, and materials we can replicate that of which we were bound ultimately to be deprived.

To the extent to which the work of Louise and her colleagues involves invisible mending, they too offer the illusion that no damage has been done. But since we see right through that illusion, what they do does not so much disguise the facts of inevitable disrepair as provide consolation for them. Elisabeth and Irene and Louise can't offer Fred's brand of consolation, for in the art world of which they are a part, it is no consolation to know that a replica of Newman's *Cathedra,* for all intents and purposes indistinguishable from the one that left his studio, might be created—by the Freds of the art world, otherwise known as forgers unless it's Newman himself. The consolation offered by the art restorers is at least twofold: that not all aspects of the inevitable aging of a work of art are unwelcome; and that given the kinds of knowledge and skills the restorers have, the decay, disintegration, or damage that is unwelcome can be undone or at least mitigated. But such consolations of repair and restoration come at a cost: The forces responsible for the welcome aging of the artwork are inseparable from those that ultimately will damage it irreparably; every attempt on the part of restorers to rescue the work of art carries not only the possibility of mutilating it but of undermining its claim to single authorship. Indeed, there wouldn't be so much concern about making sure the restorers' work can be undone if there was unassailable confidence that the repair work didn't compromise authorship.

The repaired but patently unrestored cars emerging from Willie's garage offer no illusion that time doesn't have to pass, that decay doesn't have to happen, that damage doesn't inevitably occur. But that makes the consolation Willie offers all the more powerful: It doesn't matter that things are by their nature impermanent, that they in-evitably decay or are damaged. All that matters is whether you've still got something that performs in the ways cars are supposed to perform. You needn't be bothered by the fact that due to the ravages of time the car doesn't look like it did coming off the factory floor. You can enjoy the festi-val of hybridity—the wanton mongrelization of parts, the breezy interbreeding of designer and repairer—and just not worry about tidy distinctions between automobiles and tractors, between Saabs and Volkswagens, between those who design machines and those who repair them. If Willie seems to offer no consolation, it's only because his work suggests that we don't need any.

CHAPTER 3

The Household as Repair Shop

Across the human landscape, some kind of repair or restoration or mending or rehabilitating or reconciling is bound to be going on—or at least is being considered, even if in the end rejected. But pray, who is doing all this work? Should we expect there to be a division of the labor of repair, just as we find some such division historically in almost every other human labor—are some groups or "types" of people assigned certain kinds of tasks, other such groups assigned others? Is there, for example, any repair work that has a claim to being "women's work"? Is there repair work that has been considered off limits to women? Off limits to some women but not others?

WOMEN AND THE QUESTION OF TOOLS

As we opened this broad inquiry into repair, it seemed appropriate, almost obligatory, to begin with someone like Willie, that crackerjack automobile mechanic, because the concept of repair perhaps feels most at home and most familiar in its use to describe work done on objects like cars that are part of the everyday landscape. If it's hard to imagine work that seems more quintessentially the work of repair, it's also hard to imagine a better candidate for the quintessential repairperson. It comes as no surprise that Willie is working class, white, and male, facts faithfully reflective of the several dimensions of the division of labor governing the kind of work he does. There are no doubt African American, Latino, Asian American, and Native American repairmen across the United States. But the various construction and repair trades—especially those involving skilled labor—historically have been notoriously eager to remain lily-white. And their ranks to this day include only trace amounts of women of all "races" and ethnicities, making it shocking to be reminded by some guild records from feudal England that female carpenters and saddlers were not uncommon,[1] or to learn that the circular saw was invented by a woman.[2]

Indeed, for the most part, women are much more likely to appear in pinup calendars in the offices and shops of repairmen—mechanics, plumbers, carpenters, cobblers, and so forth—than as partners in such work. Graphic and pornographic depictions of women sometimes are displayed precisely in order to make the few females on the job feel uncomfortable and unwelcome[3]—only one sign that this particular area of repair in human life (at least in a country like the United States) is brimming with anxiety about whether women can and should do such work. In both new and used bookshops it's not hard to find home repair guides addressed specifically to women.[4] It's not unusual for them to begin with a bit of a pep talk:

> The fact is that women don't have to be unhandy. They are *not* inherently nonmechanical; they have been educationally deprived by their society and then trained to believe that their aptitude is low. What is most needed is authoritative assurance that "educationally deprived" does not mean "uneducable," and that, in general, the business of making repairs is far easier than most women believe.[5]

The very existence of such books and their messages of "There's no reason you can't do this stuff too, ladies!" signal a history of women being considered unsuitable for such work, on the grounds that it is too demanding, or is something that would compromise their claim to femininity. Sometimes what slips out is an undisguised assertion of entitlement: If women take these jobs men won't have them. For example, Mary Baird, trained as a phone repair technician, reports being admonished, "You're taking a job away from a man who must provide for his wife and children."[6] Many of her male colleagues felt cramped by and resentful of her presence: "Now girly magazines had to be confined to their trucks, language had to be 'toned down' and, even worse, they had to cope with the idea that perhaps a female—who at five-foot-five and one hundred twenty pounds was clearly not an Amazon—could master *their* job."[7] There also has come to be a whole genre of writing about repair and its plethora of pleasurable accoutrements and special perks—power tools, duct tape, long trips to the hardware store—being a "guy thing" that women just don't or can't understand.

None of this, of course, means that all men are brought up to unreservedly embrace a masculinity defined in terms of skilled manual labor. It is not unusual for middle-class male white-collar professionals to think of the repair of cars or houses as perhaps something they should be able to do on the weekends but yet not choose as a career. Indeed, as Steven Gelber has shown, this version of what he has called "domestic masculinity" was on a firm footing in the United States by the 1950s.[8] A century earlier, industrialization had put many men out of the house, leaving them with scant time or incentive to develop basic skills of household maintenance and repair. But, according to Gelber, by mid-twentieth century a potent mix of forces made the possession of "do-it-yourself" skills nearly de rigueur for such men. It was both masculine—expressing mastery over tools, and yet distinctly domestic—something done around the house, perhaps in the male-defined space of a workshop. Moreover, Gelber adds, such domestic masculinity seems to have been attractive not only to middle-class homeowners, whose ordinary workweek did not involve manual labor: Do-it-yourself activities "were performed by middle-class men acting like blue-collar workers and blue-collar workers acting like middle-class homeowners."[9]

Mainstream American culture is awash in reflection on the kind of repair skills domestic masculinity is thought to include. Dave Barry, for example, has carved out a handsome career making fun of male do-it-yourselfers bumbling through home repair jobs so badly that they have to call in the professionals—the need for which, Barry wryly acknowledges, is what their wives suggested in the first place,[10] and which has spawned companies such as Rent-A-Husband.[11] Continued uneasiness about the tension between domestic masculinity and class status pops up with some regularity in the popular television program *Frasier.* In one episode, for example, Frasier and Niles Crane, who pride themselves on their Harvard educations and their extensive knowledge of Bordeaux vintages, appear to be quite embarrassed by their inability to fix automobiles and their failure to do well in night classes on car repair. But they quickly go to work banishing such embarrassment by reverting to their always-ready contempt for that kind of labor. Such disdain underscores their difference from the two working-class members of the household: from Daphne, who is thrilled by the prospect of her man Niles being able to rescue her in the breakdown lane and thereby, she says, show how much he really cares for her, and from their father, Martin, the retired cop for whom it is a momentous and very intimate act to be able to offer his tools, at long last, to his sons.[12]

But whether we focus on tool use at the workplace or in the home, we aren't likely to find many women on the scene. Perhaps the only skilled manual repair work that easily comes to mind as something that historically has fallen to women—or *some* women—to do, even if it is not entirely off limits to men, is mending clothing (and in rural fishing areas, mending nets). The profession of male tailors has a long history, and in a pinch at least some men exhibit perfectly adequate sewing skills. According to Bruce Cassiday, "Many a man in military service has had to darn a sock at a crucial time. I never yet saw such a man pretend to know how to use a needle, and yet I've watched dozens in the barracks secretly stitching rips in their clothing when they thought no one else was looking. It may have taken them longer than a woman to repair their torn clothing, but they did it!" And Una Robertson has pointed out that in early nineteenth-century Yorkshire it was commonly recognized that men as well as women knitted.[13] Still, mending family clothing seems almost always to have been the task of the women of the house (in recent Western cultures). So, even if much of what counts as ordinary repair work—in the workplace or at home —seems to have become thought of as men's and not women's work, the mending of clothing historically has been ordinary repair work that is the work of women—or at least of women whose social standing did not require that their hands remain soft and free of the evidence of labor. But is that all? Just how generic is the *Homo* in *Homo reparans*?

The case for the ubiquity of repair rests in part on the use of *repair* and its close cousins in connection with a vast and motley range of activities: fixing automobiles and mending clothing, yes, but also repairing human relationships and reweaving rips in the social fabric. When we think of repair in this larger sense, it can seem as if women spend—or, anyway, are expected to spend—an enormous amount of time doing repair work.

THE HOUSEHOLD AS REPAIR SHOP

I would like to venture that the history of the housewife—especially after industrialization isolated the household, and the women in it, from the rest of the economy[14]—suggests that women's work in the household has been to the larger society what the combined work of gas station, car wash, and repair shop is to automobiles. Though at the beginning of the twenty-first century there are severe cracks in its façade, the household (at least in what we breezily call Western industrial society) is designated as the default location for people to fuel up, get washed, clothed, and reclothed; it's where they're to receive the daily doses of repair and restoration necessary for them to keep on going, physically, mentally, emotionally, to keep on functioning as social animals (the continued importance of such tasks assigned the household is signaled by the use of the word *homeless*). Such activities, after all, have to happen *somewhere*.

Saying this doesn't require us to decide among competing views of the home as "haven in a heartless world,"[15] or as the scene of horrendous abuse and violence, or as neither haven nor horror chamber but bulwark against racist hostility and humiliation.[16] (The continuing debate over the proper description of the household is reflected in Miss Manners's recognition that if she is going to argue that the "the traditional idea of a cheerful household is worth salvaging," she has to acknowledge how hard it is for its inhabitants to control "large and small impulses that do damage to others in the household.")[17] The general idea is that whatever else it has been or has been meant to be, the household, in its nuclear and nonnuclear varieties, has had to serve as a veritable repair shop (indeed, it is against that backdrop that domestic violence seems particularly shocking).

There is first of all the repair of the human body. The body has an awesome capacity to repair itself in ways that are to the ordinary observer both visible (e.g., the healing of a cut) and invisible (e.g., the continual self-repair of DNA, or the recently discovered capacity of the human heart to repair itself).[18] But it can't do that, and will cease doing it, without being fed and watered. So, even though we might think of the feeding and watering of human beings as simple maintenance, rather than repair, such maintenance is necessary for the self-repair of the body. And that bodily repair is helped along by the knowledgeable household creation and use of salves and medicines.[19] There also is, or anyway was, the "eternal mending"[20] of clothing—absolutely crucial when there is not likely to be anything soon to replace it, whenever holes are thought inconvenient or embarrassing, or in order to keep a beloved item wearable or usable for as long as possible.

And then there is the repair necessitated by the steady flow of crises arising from the vulnerability of the human heart and from the fragility of the web of human relationships. A child is heartbroken over the death of a grandmother, or, for that matter, of a goldfish. A friendship breaks up or is slowly falling to pieces. A young person's confidence in her abilities has been shattered (this, of course, assuming that she lives in a larger context in which such confidence could have been established to begin with). The family tries to figure out how to deal with its own breakup due to separation or divorce. Children need to learn what an apology is, and when, how, and to whom to make one. They need to think about what it means to keep or break a promise. They need guidance in identifying what constitutes damage to themselves and others, aid in reflecting on what it is possible to fix, what not, what it is desirable to fix, and what not. (If Melanie Klein is right, the need for such guidance arises in humans long before it can be provided: Klein argued that babies fantasize destroying their mothers, conflate the desire with its accomplishment, and then "find support against these fears in omnipotent phantasies of a restoring kind": "If the baby has, in his aggressive phantasies, injured his mother by biting and tearing her up, he may soon build up phantasies that he is putting the bits together again and repairing her.")[21] At the same time, children may also be called upon to mend rifts in family relationships that adults can't accomplish themselves.[22]

The household functions—or is supposed to function—as a multipurpose repair site. It offers a pretty good microcosm of the variety of repair activities humans engage in, providing services on a nonprofessional basis that in many cases migrated outside the household to become the professional work of seamstresses, doctors, therapists, spiritual counselors, mediators, and judges. As Arlie Hochschild recently has argued, though "capitalism and technological developments have long been gradually deskilling parents at home,"

[t]he main "skill" still required of family members is the hardest one of all—the ability to forge, deepen, and repair relationships. Under normal circumstances the work of tending to relationships calls for noticing, acknowledging, and empathizing with the feelings of family members, patching up quarrels, and soothing hurt feelings.[23]

But relationships among family members are not the only ones that are likely to need repair, and the household perforce provides apprenticeship in such skills: Because of the variety of ways in which humans are called upon to mend themselves, others, and the relationships they are in, they need some kind of rehearsal for and training in that long before and certainly during their school years.

So, then, like cars, human beings suffer wear and tear; like cars, humans need not just maintenance but repair if they are to keep on functioning; and in the provision of such repair, the household, by default if not by design, for better and for worse, is to the larger society what the auto repair shop—along with the gas station and car wash—is to the world of automobiles. Sometimes these home repair shops do a decent job, sometimes they don't. And of course the analogy is imperfect: While apprentices in the household and in the repair shop can learn to repair, cars can't (though cars can have self-corrective mechanisms, and there are some new materials that "know" how to go back to their original shape after a collision).[24] While cars can't be violated by attempts to repair them (except in the sense that their structural integrity might be violated), there are moral constraints on our attempts to repair others, to "straighten them out" against their will. Debates over the appropriateness of corporal punishment of children, for example, are a reminder of the ongoing process of trying to determine what those constraints ought to be.

REPAIRING PEOPLE FOR WHAT?

If there is any analogy at all between the repair of automobiles and the repair of persons, we ought to be able to specify what function is being restored when the repair of persons or some aspect of them is taking place; for what makes the working on a car a matter of repair is that the function of the car or some part of it is being restored. The car now works again: It can be used to perform the function of getting its occupants relatively safely and efficiently from one place to another. But what are the functions of humans that are restored when humans are repaired? Is the household the place for the production, maintenance, and repair of humans functioning as citizens? consumers? workers? well-lubricated cogs in the social machine? all of the above?

The analogy between the repair of a car and the repair of a person suggests that there is a kind of repair of humans that restores them to a state of basic functioning, of being able to use their energies and skills as they see fit. For after all, when the mechanic restores the basic function of a car as a relatively safe and efficient moving vehicle, the idea is that the owner then can use it as she wishes. So, it would seem that just as cars are repaired so people can use them as they desire, people are repaired so that they can get back in basic working order, in order to get on with what they want to do.

But we cannot assume that repair is neutral in this sense, as we can see from the case of Willie. Willie repairs cars without regard to how they will look in their postreparative state, and to a certain extent without regard to the original design of the car. He'll get your Saab purring again like a kitten, make sure the back door opens and shuts tightly and easily, but he won't guarantee that the door he ends up using will be the same color as the rest of the car, nor will he promise not to violate the original design of the door handle or the engine. He is going to repair your car in a much different fashion than someone you hire to repair it in a way that will preserve or restore it as a particular vintage of Saab automobile. Either way, your car will once again function as a relatively safe and efficient moving vehicle. But Willie's repair is likely to complicate future attempts to restore the car as closely as possible to its original condition. Repairing a hip so that someone can walk again might under some conditions get in the way of repairing it so the person can run.

When, then, we think about the work of the household as including the repair of humans from the wear and tear of everyday life, where *repairing* means restoring them to some kind of functional state, we surely ought to ask whether repairing them to be able to function in some ways is compatible with repairing them to be able to function in others. For example, to the degree to which the household provides respite for those who work outside it from the wear and tear of that work and performs the repair necessitated by such wear and tear, it restores humans to their functions as workers. And indeed a good chunk of the scholarship on the function of the household since industrialization has been on its role in the production and reproduction of the workforce—the creation, maintenance, and, now we would add, repair of people so they are not just physically but psychologically ready and able to take on the work demanded of them, day after day after day. Under harsh conditions of labor—that is, under conditions of labor that are the norm rather than the exception in most parts of the world—the kind of maintenance and repair work done by the household resembles nothing so much as preparation for a demolition derby, in which an auto is repaired just enough so it can be entered in an event the point of which is to smash the car to smithereens. The analogy will be more or less close, depending on the extent to which workplace owners don't want to have to replace their workforce at frequent intervals.

But is repairing the worker to be able to function in the workplace compatible with repairing him or her to be able to function as citizens? They might not be incompatible, but we cannot assume that one repair suits all functions. Certainly, repairing the worker to be able to function in a destructive workplace is not the same as repairing the workplace; and it may or may not repair the worker in her struggle to make the workplace less destructive. Like all the Black girls growing up in the cotton mill town of Kannapolis, North Carolina, in the 1950s, Katie Geneva Cannon assumed she would follow her mother and become a domestic worker for white people. "[W]e were not only supposed to know how to keep house but also how to cook perfect meals and not burn food up. . . . How to mop the floors, how to pick the strings up after the mop, how to dust so that you don't break things, how to wash windows and wipe down the blinds, the whole mechanical system of how to clean a house. I knew all that by the time I was eight."[25] Because their mother was working for white families all day, Katie Cannon's sister was responsible for teaching her how to clean. Though Katie and her sisters were supposed to keep their own house in top shape— "There is nothing that would irritate a black woman more than to clean a white woman's house all day long and then come home to a dirty house"[26]—the work they did at white people's houses was, as we have learned so well from Judith Rollins and others,[27] performed in such a way and under such conditions that the superiority of the whites to the Blacks would be affirmed. "Most of the white people in Kannapolis didn't clean their houses. That was what black women were for. That was how black women would get their income, how they survived."[28] Challenging their employers in hopes of making conditions of work less toxic[29] was likely to cut off the supply of that necessary income. Katie Cannon's case is pertinent here not because she was doing repair work—indeed, cleaning house typically is thought of as maintenance, not repair, and as involving unskilled rather than skilled labor—but because some of the very good "repair work" she got at her own home was to enable her to go back day after day to damaging labor outside it.

In thinking about the household as a multipurpose repair shop, it's important to consider not only the kinds of repair that are undertaken there, but also the kinds of discussions that take place, the lessons handed down, about the varieties of damage there are in the world, what one can or can't, should or should not do about it. Indeed, there are implicit lessons in civics, morality, economics, and politics that are passed on in household discussions and decisions about to whom one has and has not to apologize, whether and how one is responsible for damage to the environment, when a marriage or partnership has frayed beyond the point of repair, what kinds of repair it is deemed appropriate for men and women of one's class or ethnicity to engage in. In certain circumstances something as seemingly simple as whether one should mend clothing is fraught with social and political significance:

> My mother always said, "A patch, my dear, is never a disgrace, but a hole . . . that is." In 1943 a neatly mended patch or a darned hole in a sock is a badge of patriotism. But no matter what the date or year—even if the threads or material do not match—a patch or a darn will always mean a badge of self-respect.[30]

Obviously, the household is not the only place where such lessons are passed on or such questions brought up. But whether households are good at it or lousy at it, they are places where people are supposed to get prepared for lives as citizens, consumers, workers, moral agents, friends. Steven Gelber reports that one of the messages given a certain class of Victorian boys was that the aggressiveness and competitiveness they'd need in the workplace would have to be learned away from the household— though paradoxically that lesson about the proper place to receive such instruction might come from the household itself.[31] One not only needs basic repair to keep functioning in the various ways demanded of us in and outside of the household; functioning in those capacities itself involves all manner of judgments about the possibility and impossibility, the desirability and undesirability, of repair. Slave testimonies and other historical sources also remind us that the household is one of the places where people are given lessons, implicitly or explicitly, about their role in the maintenance and repair or the subversion and destruction of the current social and political order: The steady maintenance and repair of white supremacy and the system of slavery, for example, required the unceasing work among whites of attempting to break the spirits and dash the hopes of slaves.[32]

The repair women do in the home—including the lessons about reparability and irreparability they explicitly or implicitly pass down—does not constitute all of their work; it is not always easily distinguishable from the rest of their work; and they are not necessarily alone in the household in doing it.[33] But they are on the whole managers by default of such repair work, whatever the size or extent of their household and however many adults there are in it. If central to domestic masculinity is the repair of material objects and the passing down of lessons about such repair, central to domestic femininity is the repair of persons and relationships, and the imparting of lessons about that kind of repair. There is no particular training for such repair, and the world outside the household may be geared to undermining it. For example, part of U.S. slavery and its legacy was the assumption that Black women working for white people should put the needs of the white families ahead of those of their own.[34]

The analogy between the household and the automobile repair shop reminds us, too, that repair can be dangerous work. It can severely hurt the repairer, and it can destroy rather than fix the object meant to be mended. Mechanics need to learn how to anticipate dangerous situations and to protect themselves, their fellow workers, and the cars in their care from the many kinds of accidents that might happen in a shop. The propane torch with which one does reparative welding could severely burn one's hand or set the car, the shop, and all its inhabitants on fire. To the extent to which women become the repairers of choice in the household—including being healers of rifts, menders of hearts—there are dangers both for them and for the other members of it. It is a crucial part of a relationship for those in it to be able to tend to its cracks and fissures themselves, to not turn automatically to a third party for a rescue operation. For example, the author of a recent book about the social and moral development of boys reports coming to recognize that when tension between him and his son got high, both he and his wife tended to rely on her to mediate, thereby not only relieving father and son of the need to figure things out on their own, but also depriving them of the chance to deepen their relationship by having to deal with fault lines in it.[35] But if the presence of a repairer-on-call threatens to stunt the growth of reparative muscle in others, it also may leave the ever reliable repairer in short supply of help when she is in need herself.

REPAIR AND THE "ETHICS OF CARE"

Carol Gilligan famously proposed some twenty years ago that there are two distinct orientations involved in conceptualizing and resolving moral puzzles and problems, one more likely to be found among men than women, the other more likely to be found among women than men. Suppose, for example, that Henry and Ruth have a fifteen-year-old daughter, Jackie. Jackie comes to her parents in tears with news that she is pregnant. Should she get an abortion?

According to an early version of the Gilliganian view, men, more likely than not, treat moral deliberation as a matter of seeking out relevant principles or rules and applying them to the case at hand. We can expect Henry to think about Jackie's predicament in terms of whether an abortion would violate, or accord with, some relevant moral law or principle. Such law provides the kind of steady compass that, on this view, is the hallmark of morality: In its absence, our moral thinking would be without proper direction, without consistency, all too partial. Unless there are rules and laws telling us what to do, we won't know how to reach a decision, we will remain without moral direction. It's the following of rules that assures us of consistency—that when another case comes along it will be treated in the same way. It's the adherence to rules that promises impartiality—that we are guided not by our current whims or fears or loves or hopes, but by the steadiness of a rule that applies no matter how we happen to feel and no matter to whom or what we happen to be attached. Wanderers in the confusing and treacherous moral wilderness need a compass—an instrument that gives clear directions, that points the same direction every day, no matter who the wanderer and no matter how much he might wish it pointed in another direction.[36]

Women, Gilligan and some of her followers appeared to argue, are likely to pose and try to resolve moral problems in quite a different way. Persons are by their very nature bound up in relation to others, and tensions and conflicts in those relations are at the heart of moral dilemmas. In order to resolve such conflicts one must focus on the specific situation of the persons involved, on the web of their relationships to people, and on how to keep those relations intact. What is the best thing for Jackie to do, given the nature of her relationship to the man involved, and her social and economic condition? How might her decision affect her relation to her parents? What kind of life would the child have? What kind of emotional and economic support does Jackie need?

Women, on this view, do not share the assumption that the proper resolution of Jackie's dilemma requires the application of a governing law or principle. Moral direction is something to be figured out by the moral travelers in the thicket of their relations with others, not something they can determine by reference to a sure and steady compass.

Attention is to be given to the specifics of Jackie's predicament, not to the ways it is like or unlike that of other girls. Jackie needs the partiality of her parents' love, not the carefully kept distance of a stone sober observer.

The first orientation, dubbed an "ethics of justice," emphasizes the autonomy of moral agents, their capacity to govern themselves and not be swayed by people around them or by powerful emotions of the moment. It insists on the importance of the ways acting from principle insures consistency and impartiality. The second, referred to as an "ethics of care," emphasizes the embeddedness and specificity of moral agents in relationships with others and embraces a kind of care for people that is unapologetically partial and apparently unconcerned with consistency across cases.

The idea that there are such distinct orientations in moral thinking, and that they map tidily onto distinctions between men and women, no matter their class, racial, or ethnic identity or their nationality, has been subject to intense scrutiny. In the ever-growing body of literature about these claims there have been probing and fruitful questions about just what ethnographic group of men and women in their early work Gilligan and associates had in mind, about whether a robust sense of justice would include care, and whether any care worthy of the name would be concerned with justice.[37] Some commentators have expressed worries that the ways women are said to care for others may reflect and strengthen their political and economic subordination to men[38] or obscure patterns of such subordination among women (for example, between female employers and the domestic workers they "care for").[39] Our interest here, however, is whether the kind of caring activity highlighted in these examinations—*whoever* engages in it—provides a window onto some of the work of *Homo reparans.* How much of what is called an "ethics of care" about repair?

The language of repair occurs hardly at all in the various discussions of what these moral orientations are, how distinct they are, and the strengths and shortcomings of each. True, it is not unusual to find reference to the maintenance of relationships—for example, women are said to "undertake to resolve conflicts by maintaining or strengthening their connections with those with whom they are in conflict";[40] their moral thinking is said to involve "a responsiveness to others that dictates providing care, preventing harm, and maintaining relationships";[41] and a reference to repair is clear in the idea that the "emotional work" women are supposed to do in the household involves "soothing tempers, boosting confidence, fueling pride, preventing fictions, and mending ego wounds."[42] But in fact there appears to be a striking similarity between the kind of knowledge and skills involved in "care ethics" thinking and those involved in doing careful repair work. Let me return for a few moments to Willie.

Though Willie has been working on Saabs, other vehicles, and farm machinery a good part of his life, he doesn't expect any two cases to be alike. He is not inclined to turn to instruction manuals or even diagnostic equipment, since as far as he is concerned they are of limited usefulness, especially compared to what he has learned about the nature of the materials he works with from long years of handling them, wrestling with them, letting them speak to him. He has intimate knowledge of the parts he deals with, the stuff of which they are made, and their actual and potential relationships to each other. This knowledge prepares him to deal with the problems his customers bring to him, but not because he sees the same problems again and again. One of the reasons he enjoys his work and that he is regarded as so skilled is that he comes up with nifty case-specific solutions to the constant stream of unique challenges.

The ethics of care highlights the intimacy of the knowledge of the moral agent as problem solver: intimate both in the sense of having or seeking specific and nuanced and contextualized knowledge of the people involved and the situations they are in, and in the sense of acknowledging or creating a close relationship to the people involved. Insofar as Ruth has a care orientation toward Jackie, she thinks of Jackie as her daughter, not just another fifteen-year-old, not just another generic human being faced with an important moral decision; she knows Jackie not just as a pregnant teenager, but as, say, someone who got involved with this young man as a way to get back at the boy she broke up with three months ago.

Willie's handling of machinery and Ruth's deliberations about Jackie call upon highly contextualized knowledge. But it is not that alone that prompts the idea that Ruth, like Willie, is doing a kind of repair work. What makes it repair work is that Jackie's world has, as we often say, fallen apart, and she needs help putting it back together again. The web of existing and future relationships that are said to be central to Ruth's thinking about Jackie's predicament is by its very nature fragile, something that is bound to need not just maintenance but repair. At the same time, unless Ruth is determined to counsel Jackie that any and all relationships need to be sustained and restored (something some critics of an ethics of care worry is being urged), Jackie is going to need help thinking about which of her relationships are possible and desirable to repair, which not: For example, what if her father says he'll disown her if she has an abortion, and her boyfriend says he'll break up with her if she doesn't? If Jackie feels shame at being pregnant and unattached, she may need help thinking about whether she can or should try to restore the picture of herself she had before the pregnancy.

Insofar as an ethics of care is about understanding people as in relationships with others, about seeing conflicts as threatening such relationships, surely a large part of moral deliberation as understood under an ethics of care is about repairing those relationships or judging that it is not possible or desirable under the circumstances to do so. If we think about the possible appropriateness of the language of repair for the kinds of situations to which an ethics of care turns our attention, it certainly looks as if the nature of the care being underscored is a concern for harms to persons, to beings understood as by their nature in breakable relation to each other. Indeed, what has been called an ethics of care implies that at the core of morality is a response to the fact of fragility, a fragility in the relationships in which and through which persons lead their lives. And then, in turn, the language of breakability, fragility, and repair suggests that one way to characterize the difference between the care and the justice orientations is that the care orientation focuses on morality as about relationships, which can collapse, whereas the justice orientation focuses on morality as about principles, the force and authority of which can be eroded. If that's the case, then it's not that care is about repair and justice isn't, but that a crucial difference between them is over where our reparative efforts ought to go—to relationships among people or to the principles by which they should live.

If we think about repair as something that must involve tools—at least the kind of tools found in hardware and plumbing supply stores or at construction sites—our cast of repair characters is mostly going to involve men. Not because all men have them or use them even if they have them, nor even because all men are supposed to have them or be able to use them: Differences in social and economic class among men are at least roughly correlated with the degree to which they use such tools to make a living. Not all working-class men make a living using such tools; still, making a living by using such tools is one version of a male working-class life. But though not all men have been welcomed into or expected to aspire to join the brotherhood of tool users, women of all classes and complexions need not even apply.

However, many repair activities don't involve such tools. It's not just cars or toilets or phone lines that break and need fixing. We humans don't just live in a world of breakables; we *are* breakables, our bodies and souls by their very nature subject to fracture and fissure. And we are social animals, our dependency upon each other given shape by the connections we find and forge among ourselves. These relationships are by their very nature subject to damage, dissolution, collapse—sometimes for the better, sometimes for the worse.

Repair work must be done on and done by humans on a more or less daily basis. Though some of that repair is taken care of without our direction or our knowledge by the miraculous mundane workings of the human organism, much of it has to be made to happen. Exploring some aspects of the lives of women has led to the suggestion that the household is a veritable repair shop. It is by default the institution for aiding and abetting the natural bodily processes of repair; for mending spirits frayed or broken by the wear and tear of life, by the damaging effects of its pleasures as well as its pains; and for providing informal lessons about the reparable and the irreparable.

CHAPTER 4

Serving Time in the Community of Repairers

Repair is at the very heart of justice—so say, anyway, proponents of the movement for restorative justice, who draw from the rich and varied palette of repair terms to express their aspirations for dealing with human conflict: repair, restoration, reconciliation, healing, mending. "Restorative justice" isn't only about fixing the flaws and making up for the imperfections in existing legal institutions; it's about putting the repair of victims, offenders, and the communities of which they are a part at the center of justice.

The language of repair in the restorative justice movement is unmistakable. Here's David Lerman, a lawyer working in the district attorney's office in Milwaukee: "Restorative Justice asks: who has been harmed; how they have been harmed; and how the offender, community, and criminal justice system can help repair the harm."[1] Those who proposed South Africa's Truth and Reconciliation Commission described its goals as including "the taking of measures aimed at the granting of reparation to, and the rehabilitation and the restoration of the human and civil dignity of, victims of violations of human rights."[2] And in current legal scholarship the restorative justice movement is described as "based on a set of values that promotes healing, repairing harm, caring, and rebuilding relationships among the victim, and offender, and the community."[3]

Perhaps, especially in comparison with familiar modes of the repair and restoration of physical objects (fixing a car, rebuilding a motorcycle, restoring a work of art), the kind of repair asked for by proponents of the restorative justice movement seems ambitious in scope—practitioners of the project hope to repair the current justice system and to turn all of us, potentially, into repairers—and lofty in its calling: Such repair is embraced as being essential to justice.

Students of repair will want to know why *H. reparans* has been called to duty in the halls of justice. But we also have to consider why in some quarters that summons has met with strong resistance: The kinds of skills we have reason to admire in repairers like Willie, Fred, and Louise and her colleagues may have analogues in the resolution of human conflicts, but that doesn't mean their exercise always will be welcome.

THE CRIMINAL JUSTICE SYSTEM
AND THE LOCUS OF REPAIR

The *restorative* in *restorative justice* is meant to signal its difference from what we know as retributive justice and to bring attention to the fact that crime and other human conflict cause damage not only to the bodies and souls of individuals but to the social fabric of communities. Proponents of restorative justice think that retributive justice systems fail to locate and properly attend to the multiple ruptures such conflict produces.

Suppose, for example, that an intruder breaks into a woman's apartment, steals her jewelry, and knocks her hard onto the floor when she comes upon him. How should he be dealt with? What is called the "criminal justice system" in Western democracies broadly understood focuses on bringing such offenders to justice by identifying the people who commit crimes and then punishing them for breaking the law.[4] It is, on the whole, retributive in nature, operating on the assumption that the appropriate way to deal with felons is to make sure they get the punishment they deserve for having broken the law. Laws—civil as well as criminal—are a crucial part of the social fabric. They allow us to live together, by protecting us from one another. Breaking the law threatens to rend the always fragile webs into which our lives are woven. Holding lawbreakers accountable for their actions stitches up the law, by repairing the assault on its authority and power over us, by restoring its place as central to the possibility of our relationships. Through the punishment he must endure, the offender pays for the damage he has done to the victims and to the social fabric of which laws are such an important part.

But there's something seriously wrong with this picture, according to restorative justice advocates, something askew in the way the current retributive system conceives of the damage crime does and the nature of the repairs it requires. True, the current criminal justice system is not without its own reparative moments: As the preceding sketch makes clear, it can be described untendentiously as involving repair. What's wrong, say the proponents of restorative justice, is that the criminal justice system fails to identify important harms—to locate all the places where repair work needs to be done—and doesn't know how to fix the harms it does identify. Yes, it is important to shore up people's confidence in a set of rules by which they are to be governed and protected. Laws are felt to exist only to the extent to which they are enforced when broken. And yes, surely the person who breaks them ought to be called upon to repair the breach. But the existing criminal justice system pays almost no attention—or the wrong kind of attention—to the victims, pays only lip service to the damage done to the community, and has abandoned any thought of punishment as reparative for the offender—in fact, it tends to treat offenders as unsalvageable or not worth repair.[5]

Proponents of restorative justice point out that the harm done the victim is not necessarily repaired by the formal endorsement of the victim's rights not to have been injured nor by the victim's knowledge that the tormentor has been punished. While the harms suffered by the victim are essential to the case brought by the representatives of the law against the offender, the law focuses on those harms only to the extent necessary to establish the guilt of the offender and the appropriate level of punishment to be meted out. There is not enough attention to the range of the injuries victims have endured or of their own understanding and assessment of them: In the previously presented example, there may be not just the physical harm done to her or her property, but the resulting fear and anxiety over the victim's loss of a sense of control over her life; victims not infrequently are stigmatized, especially in cases such as rape. Whatever work it takes to repair the multifaceted injuries victims have suffered is for the most part left up to victims themselves. The state doesn't do it; the offender is not expected to have anything to do with it; the community of which victim and offender are a part isn't really consulted except in its provision of jurors at a formal trial—members of the community with whom neither victim nor offender is supposed to have any connections.

According to the restorative justice advocate, the current criminal justice system not only fails the victim. It also ignores important needs of the communities in which crime takes place. For even if the authority and power of the laws by which a community is governed have been reaffirmed by the arrest, conviction, and incarceration (or other punishment) of offenders, not all the damage done to it has thereby been healed. Serious conflicts between and among members of the same community are rips and tears in the social fabric. They are not mended by the removal of offenders to some spot at the desolate edge or the desolate dead center of the community, nor are they mended by the struggle of victims to tend to injuries that are seen as marking them as separate from, rather than parts of, their communities. Part of the damage done to communities by the turning over of crime to experts and professionals is a loss of a sense that the community can repair itself, can figure out how to deal with conflict by itself.[6]

From the perspective of restorative justice, whatever punishing the offender accomplishes, repair does not seem its aim and even less often its product. The offender may have been punished to the full extent of the law yet remain unregenerate. It is true that historically there have been attempts to justify punishment in terms of its capacity to get offenders to mend their ways (prisons and jails as "penitentiaries," as "houses of correction"); and there have been efforts to rehabilitate prisoners while they are incarcerated, even when that has not been offered as the reason for their imprisonment. But such views have ceased to carry whatever weight they once might have had. Punishment is aimed not at repairing the harm offenders did to the victims, nor at repairing offenders or their relationships to victims and the community. Indeed, if anything, punishment seems geared to trying to break offenders and to rupture their connection to the larger society—not just by putting up all manner of physical, social, and emotional barriers, but by making offenders think that the only consequences of their acts they need to think about are the punitive consequences for themselves; offenders don't have to confront the consequences for the victims and for their community. One alternative to incarceration that some proponents of restorative justice find promising is what Australian criminologist John Braithwaite has dubbed "reintegrative shaming." Offenders appear in the courtroom in the presence of significant community members who make clear their disapproval of the offender's behavior but also shoulder responsibility for figuring out how the offender might be brought back into the fold of the community. Incarceration is treated as "a last resort, to be used for hard-core violent offenders who must be incapacitated for the safety of the community, *not* as the principal means of punishment."[7]

As proponents of the restorative justice system see it, then, the existing criminal justice system not only doesn't do the right kind of repair in the right places; it may leave victim, offender, and community in a greater state of disrepair than they were before the crime. The victim may well feel that the state is more interested in creating its own version of how she was wounded than in hers, that she has become in effect a vehicle by which the state reaffirms its own authority and power rather than the real focus of the state's concern. If the harm done to her is compounded by the way the state deals with her case in order to prosecute, well that is not the state's concern. Meanwhile, given the condition of most jails and prisons, the offender is not likely to have been "rehabilitated." Indeed, he is likely to have been left for irreparable; if poor and Black, his unsalvageability may have been presumed to be his inevitable state long before incarceration.[8]

So, then, the restorative justice movement sees itself as responding to the brute fact that the criminal justice system and the "trail 'em, nail 'em, jail 'em"[9] process by which it identifies crimes and brings perpetrators to "justice" is in a state of shambles. This is not a judgment with which restorative justice enthusiasts will find much disagreement; for example, in a recent study carried out by lawyers and criminologists from Columbia University, the system of capital punishment in the United States was pronounced "broken," so reeking of incompetence and unfairness that "[t]he time is ripe to fix the death penalty. Or, if it can't be fixed, to end it."[10] But the concern of restorative justice proponents is not that often associated with the political right—that stricter law enforcement is necessary. Nor is it that often heard from the political left—that the system is deeply flawed inasmuch as it systematically reflects and perpetuates class, ethnic, and racial discrimination, the kind that shows up in the everyday example of a department store's security agent treating the well-dressed white shoplifter much more leniently than her black teenage counterpart.[11] The restorative justice movement focuses neither on how many criminals are caught nor on how the dragnet of the law is constructed to capture and punish some people rather than others. Neither of these criticisms gets at what proponents of the restorative justice movement find fundamentally troubling about the criminal justice system: its failure to understand and properly locate the nature of the harms done and to institute appropriate procedures for repairing those harms.

RESTORATIVE JUSTICE AND THE
COMMUNITY OF REPAIRERS

The restorative justice approach not only hopes to bring attention to the multiple locations of the wounds inflicted by a criminal act; it aims to involve all those affected by that act in the work necessary to carry out the appropriate repairs. Successful repair requires knowing what the actual damages are. So, the victim is called upon to describe as best she can the nature of the harms she has suffered, in order to make clear just what needs repairing. The offender learns in detail about the consequences of his action, about the nature of the damage he has done. The community does its best to provide a forum in which such revelation and recognition can take place, to provide a context in which some kind of reconciliation between the parties can occur and in which they can be integrated back into the community. Victim, offender, and community work together to develop an understanding of what work by the offender would constitute repair of the damages he has caused. They are to be thought of as partners in repair, not adversaries.

To get some idea of the ways in which all parties to a conflict become participant repairers of it, we can look at two quite different projects: the highly publicized, much-commented upon Truth and Reconciliation Commission in South Africa, and a modest program in the district attorney's office in Milwaukee, Wisconsin.

The mandate of the Truth and Reconciliation Commission (TRC) was to find a way for South Africa to break with its apartheid past without forgetting about that past but also without having its legacy of violence, hatred, fear, and distrust continue to exert such a powerful influence in relationships among Blacks, whites, and coloureds in the new democratic regime. The TRC, which began its work in earnest in 1996 and produced a Final Report in 1998, aimed to satisfy the deep and desperate longings of apartheid's victims to find out what happened to their loved ones, to have apartheid's henchmen and -women own up to what they had done, but without that knowledge making a continued life together impossible. Victims were invited to give accounts of what happened to them and their families and communities. Those willing to tell the truth in public about the crimes they committed in the service of the apartheid government were not to be thrown into prison but to gain amnesty and resume full citizenship. Part of what animated the TRC was the belief that neither the victims nor the larger society could know what it was recovering from or be given the tools to recover in the absence of such revelations. The victims' rights might have been honored and respected by the harsh punishment of their oppressors, but backers of the TRC, such as Archbishop Desmond Tutu, believed that the retribution made possible through adversarial law would not have helped victims deal with the ways in which their lack of knowledge compounded their grief, nor been able to offer the dignity afforded victims in being able to ask the kinds of questions they wanted to ask. It would not have assisted the larger society in coming to acknowledge what had happened, aided them in summoning the commitment to create a different kind of nation.

Proponents of the TRC believed that the healing necessary for individuals and the nation could not be accomplished by the ordinary tribunals of justice—and not just because those tribunals themselves were likely to still carry the disease of apartheid or because they might be used by the victors to exact revenge. For proponents of restorative justice, even retributive systems at their best just can't accomplish the complex and multifarious repair work that so much of human conflict involves. Retribution might be a partner to restoration—the work of the TRC did not preclude prosecution and punishment for those charged with criminal activity who remained unwilling to confess or unable to convince the TRC that their crimes were politically as opposed to personally motivated—but the retributive response was thought (by the TRC's proponents, if not its critics)[12] to be a distant second best to the restorative one.

Champions of restorative justice don't point only to very prominent and public examples such as the TRC (versions of which have been or are beginning to be put in place around the world, in Nigeria, Panama, Sierra Leone, East Timor; serious consideration of them is taking place in Mexico, Bosnia, Serbia, Ghana, Burundi, and Canada).[13] Legal activists and scholars tend to point to much more modest examples as evidence that restorative justice in their countries has become part of the mainstream.

David Lerman, a lawyer with the Milwaukee County District Attorney's Office for more than ten years and a very active advocate of the restorative justice movement, cites the following case—rather mundane in comparison with the case of a postapartheid South Africa—as "a great example of Restorative Justice at work": A young woman cashiering at a grocery store is caught taking money from the till—enough money, in fact, to convict her of a felony. But Milwaukee's Victim–Offender Conferencing program allowed the store representatives and the young woman to settle the matter outside of court. Both parties agreed to a meeting during which they went over what happened, talked through the impact her actions had had, and together worked out "how to repair the harm caused by the act."[14] In addition to the offender and the store representatives, the conference included a lawyer for the offender, two trained facilitators, and two members of the community belonging to a local group called the Task Force on Restorative Justice. The young woman confessed and apparently was both remorseful and embarrassed. The agreed upon repair work included not only restitution of the money but a commitment to talk with new employees about what she had done and what had happened to her. The local prosecutor was not entirely out of sight, indeed was ready to prosecute if she failed to keep her promises. But the offender, her victims, and the community had much more to say about the nature of the harms inflicted and the best ways of repairing them than they would have had the case been prosecuted in the "normal" retributive way.

Whatever else one thinks of these restorative justice projects—we shall turn in a few minutes to some of the worries they have engendered—it certainly is clear that the envisioned repair work is likely to require knowledge and skills not so widely called upon in the criminal justice system as presently constituted. In the words of the Law Commission of Canada:

> In a restorative justice framework, the purpose of the criminal justice system is to respond to the harms caused by the conflict. This requires a complete understanding of the relationship between the victim and the wrongdoer, the nature of the conflict, the full range of harms that the victim received, what can be done to repair the harm and an understanding of what prompted the offender's behaviour and what can be done to prevent this behaviour from occurring in the future.[15]

Such knowledge, we can well imagine, is not easy to come by; it is likely to be painfully gained; it requires that all do their best to tell the truth. Insofar as it doesn't involve the ready invocation of rules and principles, it requires all involved to think flexibly and creatively. Such understanding and skill are what people must turn to when the model under which they are working is not one in which "parties to a conflict are constituted as legal subjects with rights" but "individuals with problems that need to be solved,"[16] when the context is one in which "crime is considered primarily as a wrong against another person and secondarily as a wrong against the state."[17]

From the perspective of the restorative justice movement, the extent to which we seem ill-prepared to engage in such repair work—whether as victims, offenders, or community members—is a measure of our having lived for so long in societies where the assumption is that crime is to be dealt with solely as a violation of someone's rights and should be handled by the proper legal authorities, who are charged with finding the guilty party and punishing him or her appropriately. It's a measure of our having left undeveloped our capacity to deal with conflict independently of the formal legal system. Though restorative systems of justice have long been familiar to some tribal communities in Africa, Australia, the United States, and Canada,[18] mainstream law has evolved in ways that have kept most people from developing the kinds of knowledge and skills needed to properly understand the damage that needs attending to, the creativity it takes to think about how best to do the repairs, and the abilities to carry them out.

JUSTICE AS REPAIR

Proponents of restorative justice offer it up not as a formal theory of justice but as a model of how individuals and institutions in and outside the law can work together to most effectively and thoroughly repair the multiple harms infraction of civil and criminal law entails. When justice is "restorative," it responds to the wrongs inflicted by one party on another by restoring "social equality in relationships—that is, relationships in which each person's rights to equal dignity, concern and respect are satisfied."[19] Its focus is not directly on systematic inequalities based on race, ethnicity, gender, or class, though it recognizes the complex ways in which those can get played out in the commission of crime and in the treatment of victims and offenders. Rather, its immediate concern is on the relationships among those most directly involved in the conflict—the victim, the offender, and the community. From the vantage point of restorative justice, justice in any robust sense is not served if, after a crime, all that happens is that someone is found guilty and then punished, even if the process is fair and the punishment seems in proper proportion to the crime. Restorative justice doesn't hesitate to assign responsibility for the wrongful deed, but it is deeply skeptical about punishing the person through incarceration or any other form of painful or isolating treatment that does nothing to repair the parties to the crime or the relationships among them. The wrongdoer will "pay for misdeeds" by engaging in reparative activities (which can include but are not limited to the return of stolen goods or property), the details of which are to be derived not from penal codes but from negotiations among the victim, the offender, and the community. Proponents of restorative justice are not unconcerned about procedural safeguards such as fairness of treatment and proportionality in sentencing, but details of how those get folded into negotiations are to be derived from the participants' sense of what justice in the particular case requires, not from some set of abstract formulas. The idea is not so much making punishment proportional to the crime but doing repairs appropriate to the various harms inflicted. The overriding aims are the restoration of social equality among the participants, not the retributive punishment of the offender; the reintegration of both victim and offender into the community, not their isolation.

Justice thus comes to be articulated in the language of repair, restoration, healing, reconciliation. Justice is achieved when the requisite repairs are accomplished—the healing of the victim, the return of the offender to the fold after doing the necessary repair work, the rifts in the community mended. We can tell whether justice has been done not by checking to see whether certain principles have been applied, or whether the offender has gotten his or her just deserts. For justice, on this view, involves "a mediating and negotiating process rather than a process of applying rules and imposing decisions."[20] Justice understood in this way is rather like medicine. When an injustice is done, both victim and community are wounded and need to be healed. The offender's participation is seen as necessary to such repair, and through that process his or her standing in the community is restored. The proper remedy is not to remove offenders further from the community but to have them participate directly in the repair of the victim and of the community.

As proponents of restorative justice themselves point out, the model of retributive justice is so familiar to many of us that we have little experience in or training for carrying out the ambitious and demanding repair work restorative justice proposes we undertake. But still: Is it really the case that the only way to repair the criminal justice system is to make us all, potentially, into small collectives of repairers?

Restorative justice enthusiasts point to past and present

examples of restorative justice projects at work as ample evidence that they certainly are possible. Indeed, according to some legal historians, legal systems based on retributive justice are the anomaly across time and cultures; restorative justice "has been the dominant model of criminal justice throughout most of human history for all the worlds' people."[21] For example, Danielle Allen has argued that in classical Athens wrongdoing was seen as a kind of "communal disease," and responses to it were expected to attend to disrupted relations among members of the community.[22] In legal systems based on the English model, the movement toward retributive justice did not begin until the eleventh or twelfth century, and it wasn't until the nineteenth century that the state, or the crown, had successfully arrogated to itself the authority and power to condemn and punish offenders.[23] Until that time retribution was not the norm but resorted to with regret and only after conflict resolution within communities failed. In many precolonial African societies, it is said, offenders were dealt with much more along the lines of a restorative justice rather than a retributive justice model: The aim of the proceedings was to help out victims and to restore harmony within the community.

Justice was not associated with punishment but with *ubuntu,* an African concept—invoked in the development of the Truth and Reconciliation Commission in South Africa—that focuses on an interconnectedness of people that makes harm to any harm to all. In a somewhat similar fashion David Lerman claims that in the U.S. context, "Restorative Justice brings the law back to its primary purpose of creating and ensuring the continuation of a community."[24] In any event, programs have been proliferating across the United States, Canada, Australia, and New Zealand over the past twenty to thirty years. The American Bar Association has endorsed the use of victim–offender mediation programs,[25] and according to a recent count, there were at least 700 such programs in Europe, 300 in the United States, 26 in Canada.[26] Both U.S. Supreme Court Justice Sandra Day O'Connor and Janet Reno, attorney general under President Bill Clinton, have expressed enthusiasm about nonadversarial resolutions of conflicts that focus less on punishment and deterrence and more on healing both parties to the conflict and the communities of which they are a part.[27]

Such confidence in the workability of restorative justice projects hardly reassures many of the movement's critics; on the contrary, it heightens their concern. Proponents of restorative justice rely on the language of repair to describe the nature of the work and by implication the kind of workers that justice requires. Though critics of such projects don't put it this way, much of what concerns them can be seen as worries that features of repair and restoration perfectly appropriate in dealing with material objects may not be appropriate in dealing with human beings.

IMPROVISATORY REPAIR AND THE PROBLEM OF FAIRNESS

Critics of restorative justice worry that certain protections built into the formal structure under which the present criminal justice system operates may be lost in the informal settings in which conflicts are resolved along the lines of restorative justice protocols. Whatever else justice requires, surely it requires that similar cases be treated similarly: It's just not fair if Betty gets a lighter sentence than Bob when each was caught stealing roughly the same amount from the till. The existing criminal justice system can be criticized for its failure to live up to the ideal of consistency (e.g., assaults on white victims are prosecuted much more ferociously than those on Blacks), but that is the point: The ideal is there to use as a tool of criticism.

Consistency, however, does not seem to be an ideal in restorative justice: The goal is to repair the harms, whatever form those repairs the ad hoc ensemble of repairers determine in an ad hoc fashion to be appropriate. Recall that restorative justice casts participants not as "parties to a conflict . . . constituted as legal subjects with rights" but as "individuals with problems that need to be solved"; that restorative justice involves "a mediating and negotiating process rather than a process for applying rules and imposing decisions." This is the source of critics' worry that defendants will be deprived of rights to be treated fairly: What's to guide the problem-solving session, or negotiations, or mediating process? Legal precedent does not have to be consulted, and the participants in the reparative process are likely to have little experience in this particular kind of problem solving. Proponents of restorative justice celebrate how parties to a conflict need to be creative, flexible, and practical, while critics see these features as invitations to improvisation and arbitrariness.

The improvisatory character of repair that we explored in the case of Willie can help illuminate the kind of worries some critics have about the reparative impulse in the restorative justice movement. The creativity we admire in Willie isn't necessarily welcome in other contexts. Recall that the conditions under which Willie works require and thus license his finding creative solutions to unique problems. Willie has said of the cars and trucks and other machinery his neighbors bring to him for repair that no two cases are the same: " 'Things are broken or worn in different ways—they each have their own characteristics.' "[28] Willie doesn't think that it will be useful for him to turn to either repair manuals or diagnostic equipment to solve the particular problems posed by the flawed or damaged machinery that ends up in his shop. He certainly is not bound by the procedures such resources suggest. And he is free to do the repairs in any way he can devise; all that matters is whether the car runs relatively safely and efficiently. Nobody is going to complain if he fixes the broken door in one Saab one way, and the broken door in another Saab in some other fashion. If the task is to repair what's broken, to fix what's not working, concerns about "fairness" don't arise. (We are not speaking here, of course, about whether Willie's clients are treated fairly—for example, about whether it would be fair for him to charge the same amount for a two-hour and a twenty-two-hour repair of the same engine problem.)

Willie's particular skills as a repairperson include his ability to improvise. Reparative improvisation, like musical improvisation, involves making things up as you go along, not necessarily repeating what has come before and not worrying about similarities between this improvisation, the ones you've done before, and the ones you'll create in the future. This, of course, does not mean that Willie's reparative improvisations are free of rules or constraints. Willie has to know how to use tools properly and understand the kinds of stresses and strains different materials can withstand, just as musicians have to know how to play their instruments and recognize the difference between improvisation, which occurs in a given musical context, and utterly random or arbitrary sound making. Improvisation of all kinds takes discipline and skill. But by definition, improvisation involves doing something different from what you did the last time a similar occasion arose. Jazz musicians seek out improvisatory moments; Willie doesn't necessarily seek them out, but the nature of his work ends up presenting him with such challenges, which in his case is one of the reasons he enjoys the work.

So, one way to put a concern of critics of restorative justice is that its proponents mistakenly think that justice can be served by improvisatory repair. But to the extent that the repairs proposed really are improvisatory, they appear to be at odds with a basic requirement of justice: that similar cases are to be treated similarly.

RESTORATION AND THE PROBLEM OF THE *STATUS QUO ANTE*

The notion of restoration at the heart of the restorative justice movement has sent chills down the spines of some critics, who point out that restoration strongly suggests a return to an earlier state. What is sacred about that earlier state? Couldn't it in fact be a state in which at least one and probably more of the parties to a conflict were being abused or exploited or otherwise mistreated? For example, should any woman be encouraged to restore a relationship with a partner who regularly assaulted her?

Concerns of this sort might be clarified by thinking again about the restorative efforts of Fred Haefele. His rebuilding of a classic motorcycle was animated by a desire to replicate something that had existed in the past. He treated the original design as if it were sacred: No questions were to be asked about it, no changes made to it, even despite what Fred recognized as potentially dangerous safety flaws. If some critics of restorative justice worry that the kind of repair it has in mind is too Willie-like, too improvisatory, too unconcerned about precedent to serve as a model for a system of justice concerned with fairness, others worry it that it is too Fred-like, that the proposed projects of restoration are too much in thrall to the past, that they preclude criticism of the state of affairs they wish to restore.

REPAIR AND THE ARROGANCE OF CORRECTION

Some of the fiercest critics of the restorative justice movement are concerned about an asymmetry in the locus of proposed repairs: that while in the case of the victim the aim is to repair *her situation,* in the case of the defendant, the aim is to fix *him*. Assessments of the success of the repairs will be based on how the victim *feels,* yet at the same time on how much the defendant has fundamentally *changed:* she gets asked if she is in a better state, but he is checked out to see whether he has become a better person. She'll be asked if her body and soul have mended; he'll be examined to see if his person has been fixed, been corrected.[29]

A striking contrast between the work of Willie and Fred, on the one hand, and Elisabeth, Louise, and Irene, on the other, is instructive in this connection. Recall that as different as the work of Willie and Fred is in some respects, both are free to do to the objects in their care whatever is necessary to get them to the desired point of repair or restoration. It doesn't matter to Willie or his customers what the repaired car looks like or how much Willie might alter the original design; Fred is not allowed to fiddle in any way with the original design, but there are no constraints on what he might do to the now pretty well rotten original parts, as long as whatever he does serves the aim of replicating a machine fresh off the factory floor. Louise and her co-conservators, however, must keep their handiwork to an absolute minimum. They certainly can't, like Willie, use whatever paint happens to be available to restore the Newman artwork; but neither can they, like Fred, scrape off any existing paint and start all over again in order to replicate the Newman. The Newman painting has an integrity and identity as a Newman work of art that must be respected and would be destroyed by attempts to improve upon or rebuild the painting.

The particularly narrow constraints under which art restorers are expected to operate remind us that repair is a significant intervention in the career of an object, representing a decision somewhere by somebody that there is a flaw or a break or some kind of damage and that such flaw or break or damage should not be left unattended. But just because something is broken or damaged doesn't mean it should be fixed or that anyone and everyone is entitled to fix it. Such cautionary reminders seem even more to the point when there is a question of repairing a human being. If it is a fair characterization of the existing criminal justice system that it regards its prisoners as irreparable beings, best left warehoused in institutions until they rot away, is it also a fair characterization of the restorative justice system that it regards offenders as ripe for repair, to be subject to any processes that will turn them into law-abiding citizens? Some of the movement's critics have such worries.

DEMOCRACY AND THE NECESSITY OF SPUTTERING

Another concern voiced by critics is that restorative justice projects in effect confuse the desirability of keeping people from harming each other with the desirability of snuffing out all conflict. Some wonder, for example, whether victim–offender mediation programs in the United States are premised on the assumption that conflict is pathological,[30] whether the language of mediation and repair depoliticizes struggles between those at the center and those at the margins of political, social, and economic power, obscuring the possibility that law breaking sometimes represents resistance to oppressive institutions. Some of the critics of South Africa's Truth and Reconciliation Commission have asked whether the goal of achieving reconciliation among Blacks, whites, and coloureds in a postapartheid South Africa will preclude the robust kinds of disagreement that are bound to characterize any democracy worthy of the name.

> Reconciliation is an illiberal aim if it means expecting an entire society to subscribe to a single comprehensive moral perspective. . . . In the democratic politics that the new South Africa seeks, a substantial degree of disharmony is not only inevitable but desirable. It can be both a sign and a condition of a healthy democracy.[31]

There is, in short, anxiety in some quarters about whether the ready importation of the language of repair and restoration as a response to human conflict misleadingly invites us to think of democracies as things that ought to run smoothly, of groups within democracies as seamlessly joined together, of there being a social fabric the inevitable rips and tears to which should be quickly mended. After all, we are supposed to judge the success of Willie's repair jobs by reference to how smoothly, efficiently, and safely the car runs. And while Willie's repairs are fully compatible with the car's having its motley history written into and all over it, its hybrid ancestry unapologetically exposed, Fred's rebuilt motorcycle is a celebration of purity and homogeneity, a result achieved by the refusal to incorporate inauthentic parts and through an erasure of the machine's actual history. And then there is the small miracle performed by Elisabeth, Irene, and Louise, the invisible mending that allows visitors to forget that the work of art ever was ripped. Repair and restoration represent a decision that damage and decay are not to be tolerated. Engines should run smoothly. Parts should be of the same stock and fit together beautifully. Rips should be mended in such a way as to suggest that they never were there in the first place. But in the eyes of some of the critics of restorative justice, democracy is not about efficiency, harmony, and homogeneity and should not tolerate attempts to cover over the history of conflict. While democracy cannot function if citizens are constantly embattled, endlessly engaged in deadly and disruptive violence, it also cannot function if the ending of all disagreement, tension, and conflict through repair, restoration, and reconciliation takes over its animating center.

Students of *H. reparans* can't help noting the enthusiasm with which advocates of restorative justice embrace the family of repair terms; we can't help being struck by the hope and confidence they have in the reparative knowledge and skills of potentially all of us as ordinary citizens. In linking repair and its sister activities to justice, the movement suggests there is a kind of repair that is both a lofty and noble calling and yet one that is available to, perhaps obligatory for, all of us. But it is that very enthusiasm for repair and restoration and reconciliation that worries the movement's critics. This will not be the last time we'll be reminded that being the repairing animal means being called upon to judge and do battle over when, where, and how the reparative impulse is to be indulged—be it in the garage, the museum, or the halls of justice.

CHAPTER 5

In the Toolbox:
Words and Money

Apology and monetary reparations are decidedly different instruments we've devised to repair some of the injuries we're wont to inflict upon each other. Reparations mean never having to say you're sorry. Indeed, that is one of the reasons why monetary reparations by themselves seem an inadequate way to recognize and respond to the kinds of harms visited on some human beings by others. Such payments seem harsh and unfeeling, to suggest that whoever and whatever was damaged can be repaired or restored with cold cash. No sorrow need be expressed, no offer of forgiveness need be contemplated. Not only is there nothing money can't buy, there is nothing money can't fix.

This feature of reparations is why it is not unusual to find both apologies and reparations requested in movements to redress serious and devastating harms—injuries such as those incurred by members of decimated Native American and First Nations communities in the United

States and Canada; by slaves and their descendants in the United States; by survivors of the Japanese American internment camps and their families; and by victims and their close relatives of the Nazi Holocaust, to name a few prominent examples. Apologies and reparations seem to complement each other in just the right ways, reparations testifying to the sincerity of an apology, apology providing evidence of a sense of personal responsibility for damages the cost of which reparations help defray.

It is perhaps easy to imagine why perpetrators of injustice might prefer to avoid the self-indictment entailed in a sincere apology's expression of sorrow and regret for having harmed another. But by way of examining the difference between apology and reparations as modes of repair, we shall here explore the possibility that the emotional coolness of reparations is precisely why victims of injustice might not welcome apology, why groups who have endured systematic injustice might seek reparations unaccompanied by expressions of sorrow, regret, and other likely ingredients of the emotional tableaux associated with apology. Such a view has not been put forward explicitly by anyone arguing for reparations, though it is implicit in Randall Robinson's recent book on reparations for African Americans in the context of U.S. slavery and its aftermath. And, as we shall also see, it seems implicit in James Baldwin's understanding of the history of Black/white relations. In any event, exploring such a view turns out to tell us about the difference but also the connection between the knowledge and skills *H. reparans* needs to apologize and those required for carrying out reparations.

REPARATIONS

Though sometimes those arguing for reparations for African Americans have included policies and programs such as affirmative action, the term is used here as James Foreman did in the Black Manifesto 1969,[1] and as Randall Robinson does in his recent book *The Debt:*[2] reparations as monetary payments to African Americans for unpaid labor during slavery, for the systematic exploitation of Black labor since then, for the denial to Blacks of access to ordinary forms of investment in real estate and other instruments of possible long-term security.[3] We won't deal explicitly with questions about the moral and legal foundations for such claims or the formulas by which the damages would be calculated. Our focus is on what monetary reparations accomplish and how they accomplish it, on what is required of both those who have to pay the reparations and those who receive them.

What is extracted of payers of reparations? Cash or its equivalents, of course, but what else? By definition, the payers are those charged with making the payments, and whether or not they actually caused the damages for which payments are now being made, they are those through whom an attempt is being made to right a wrong. Even if those responsible for the payments are also the guilty party, neither an admission of such guilt nor an expression of sorrow or regret for their deeds is necessary in order for the reparations to be achieved. The reparations process has determined that a certain sum is due the payees; the payers have only to produce that sum. It doesn't matter whether they feel remorse for their actions, indignation at being charged with responsibility for the damages, resentment toward the authorities compelling them to pay or toward the payees, despair over the new state of their finances, or anything else. The necessary transaction as such extracts nothing from them other than money, whatever their emotions happen to be.

There are some important respects in which the emotions of those receiving the payments cannot similarly be disregarded. Part of the final tally may well include a calculation of the emotional and spiritual damage done to those who have suffered injustice, a reckoning in monetary terms of the value of dignity and self-respect. Such a tally may reflect an understanding that, though matters of the mind and heart cannot be reduced to or expressed merely in terms of money, payments must somehow recognize the long-term effects of daily humiliation and shattering of hope, of the deliberate denial of the comforts of family and community. Tort law in the United States has long recognized emotional pain and suffering and has required payment of damages as a form of redress.[4] Lawyers filing wrongful death claims for dependents of the September 11 victims—at the World Trade Center, the Pentagon, and on the hijacked planes—include in their calculations not only the value of the victims' expected incomes but the suffering endured by the victims while dying and—at least in some states—the dependents' grief, anguish, and loss of companionship.[5]

Nonetheless, the recipients of reparations are under no

obligation to have or express any particular emotion toward the payers or toward the intermediaries who exact the reparations. They are not bound to feel gratitude for the institutions that make reparations possible, nor to those who pay them. Their being entitled to and receiving reparations has no bearing on the appropriateness or inappropriateness of whatever emotions they have had and continue to have about what they have had to endure. If there is any case to be made for their giving up resentment, it can have nothing to do with their having received reparations. If reparations means from the side of the payers not having to say you're sorry, it also means from the side of the payees not being called upon to forgive, not being pressed to forgo resentment.

APOLOGY

In order to apologize—really apologize, and not just utter some words—for something one has done or failed to do, one has not only to acknowledge responsibility for but express sincere sorrow and regret over this action or inaction. One can apologize only for acts for which one has no excuse:[6] If one has an excuse, there is nothing to apologize for, even if there is something to feel sorry about ("I'm sorry that you are hurt," even "I'm sorry that my actions hurt you," is quite different from "I'm sorry that I hurt you"). A genuine apology thus involves a rather raw exposure of the apologizer: Having done the deed, one now not only reiterates having done it, but strips away any suggestion that there are extenuating circumstances that could relieve one of blame; it must be clear that he regrets what he has done and feels sorrow over what he has wrought. He doesn't just wish things were otherwise; he fully acknowledges his role in bringing them to this sorry state. Moreover, apology is inappropriate if what one has done does not really constitute damage. If what I have done to you is something to be apologized for, it must be something that harms you. But the damage does not stop there; my action also jeopardizes the relationship between us and threatens to undermine an implicit or explicit social rule about how we are to behave toward each other. To the degree to which the maintenance of such rules is crucial to preventing rips in the larger social fabric, the damage I've done also threatens to ripple beyond our particular relationship.[7]

In short, sincere apology is deeply personal, both in bringing attention to one's person—*mea* culpa—and in laying bare one's emotions. It is revelatory of significant beliefs and commitments, announcing one's investment in the rules by which our relationships with others are governed, and acknowledging that I and those I've harmed are joint members of the community governed by such rules. To apologize to someone is to say that there is a harm worth attending to, a relationship worth mending, a rule worth honoring, a community worth preserving.

While one can apologize for denying or defrauding people of income that is rightly theirs, such an apology itself is not a monetary transaction and cannot be reduced to one. Money can legally be extracted from those who engage in such fraud, whatever the defrauders happen to feel about the laws under which they are charged, the people they harm, and the larger community. But if the defrauders sincerely offer an apology for what they've done, then we learn something significant about them and what they care about.

We saw that in the case of reparations neither the emotions of the payers nor those of the payees (except for purposes of calculating damages) are relevant. The emotions of apologizers are crucial to the genuineness of the apology. What about the emotions of those to whom the apology is offered?

The apology itself is the work of the apologizer. The one to whom the apology is offered can threaten the execution of the apology if she disagrees with the description of that for which the apology is offered ("You didn't just damage my car, you caused me whiplash!"), but otherwise she plays no role in the formulation and performance of the apology. She's not the one who acknowledges her misdeeds and her sorrow over having committed them. Indeed, the more she plays a role in the production of the apology—for example, the more she has to prompt it—the less certain we might be that it is sincere.

And yet once the apology is offered, it hangs there, waiting for a response from the one to whom it is offered. The vulnerability of the apologizer, the rawly personal quality of the apology, strongly invites, even if it does not require, a personally revealing response from the one to whom it is offered. Since apologies cannot be forced from people—the very fact of their being forced undermines their claim to sincerity—and since they involve a form of self-incrimination (of the sort it is the purpose of the Fifth Amendment of the U.S. Constitution to protect its citizens from), an apology is a kind of offering, a kind of gift. An apology voluntarily offers up information about one's deeds that might be quite difficult to establish otherwise and information about one's feelings about those deeds, which simply underscore one's culpability. Silence is—but does not seem—an option for the person to whom the apology is offered; she is no less part of the relationship than the apologizer, no less a member of a community governed by certain rules; and what she does with the apology offered her has as much an effect on that relationship and that community as what the apologizer does. The repair that apology tries to carry out cannot be accomplished only by the apologizer. An apology is an invitation to share in a ritual of repair, in a dance that takes more than one dancer.

Indeed, forgiveness might be seen as a willingness not just to acknowledge the invitation to dance but to accept it, give it a whirl, to engage with a partner, even if warily. One party's offer of an apology is an attempt to repair the damage he inflicted on the other. He broke or weakened the connection between them, pulled hard at the fabric holding the larger community together, but the damage cannot be mended by his apology alone; without the forgiveness of the injured party, the relationship cannot be repaired. That's one of the differences between fixing inanimate objects and mending human relationships: The car you wrecked doesn't need your forgiveness in order to be fixed (though it may for other reasons be irreparable, might, in fact, like other objects, sometimes be described metaphorically as "unforgiving"). Human relationships are such that they can be broken by one party but can't be repaired without both parties. Apology imposes a kind of responsibility on the one to whom it is offered: Though he had nothing to do with the rending of the relationship, now that the culprit has apologized and thus done his part in attempting to restore it, the intended recipient finds himself being called upon to complete the circle of repair.

Sincere apology requires and thus exposes certain emotions in the apologizer. But in putting into play an established ritual of repair, it ends up being revelatory of the emotions of the injured party as well. Of course, in one sense we must already have some idea of the injured party's emotion if the act warrants apology: Most harms deserving apology involve some kind of harm that registers emotionally—humiliating other people, making them angry, making them frightened, crushing their hearts, dashing their hopes. And the apology itself is likely to contain a reference to such feelings: "I am sorry I have caused you such grief."

But in its invitation to complete the mending, apology opens up the question of the injured party's emotions in yet another way: for the question naturally arises as to whether the injured party forgives the one who has injured her, and that question cannot be answered unless we know whether she continues to feel resentment or not. (If she didn't originally feel resentment over the act for which an apology is now being offered, she wouldn't even think the apology appropriate—"there is nothing to apologize for.") Once the apology is proffered, the spotlight turns on the one to whom it is addressed: Will she or won't she give up her resentment? Even in the absence of an apology, there is likely to be great pressure to give up resentment. As Jean Améry learned while trying to figure out how to recover from his treatment at the hands of Nazi soldiers and their sympathizers, there may well be attempts to shame one out of resentment, insinuations that people who hold on to resentment are either emotionally unhealthy —suffering from "concentration camp syndrome"—or morally small—harboring pathetic and unrealistic visions of revenge. They are charged with refusing to let time heal their wounds, with holding so tightly to their resentment that they are unable or unwilling to do their share of the continuous repair work that makes human society possible.[8] If there is pressure to give up resentment even in the absence of apology, surely, or so it would seem, there is even more pressure when a sincere apology has been put on the table.

The scene of apology, then, is by its very nature emotionally charged. It is impossible in the absence of sorrow and remorse in the one who apologizes. At the same time, apology presupposes hurt and resentment in its recipient and is incomplete in the absence of some emotional change in her as a result of the apologizer's admission of guilt and expression of sincere regret.

SLAVERY AND APOLOGY

President Bill Clinton wasn't responsible for the horrors inflicted on the Black men whose syphilis intentionally went untreated during the four decades of the Tuskegee

Study (the 1930s to the 1970s). But in 1997, as president of the United States, he apologized to the survivors and their families: "We can look you in the eye and finally say on the behalf of the American people: What the United States did was shameful, and I am sorry."[9] There are no conceptual problems with a president of the United States, or anyone else vested with the authority to speak on behalf of "the American people" or some portion of them, offering an apology for slavery or its legacies such as the Tuskegee Study. (Indeed, Clinton's apology could serve as a model for a more general apology for slavery were one forthcoming.) There are some differences between one person apologizing to another for harm she has done her and a representative of a group apologizing to another group,[10] but they don't affect the logical possibility of an apology for slavery. The question here is not whether it is possible but whether it is desirable.

Given the characteristics of apology that have emerged so far, an apology from the president or some other appropriate representative of the U.S. government for slavery and its complex legacy would seem on the face of it to be quite desirable to those also seeking reparations. If it were to resemble President Clinton's apology in connection with the Tuskegee Study, such an apology would not be vague or evasive in its description of the nature of the injuries and injustices apologized for. It would be capacious in its acknowledgment of the range of harms inflicted, including but not limited to damages to health, earning power, dignity, and self-worth. The apology would acknowledge to the appropriate extent the responsibility of the U.S. government for supporting or condoning actions and institutions that were/are harmful to African Americans in the ways specified previously; no attempt would be made to excuse or explain away such actions, nor to underplay the extent to which they were/are the manifestations of racism. It would underscore the shared status of whites and Blacks as joint and equal members of a community of moral agents.

If, as so many of slavery's defenders insisted, Blacks were not capable of suffering in the ways and to the degrees that whites were, if, as some further claimed, slavery actually was good for Blacks, then there would be no reason to apologize for slavery. If there are good reasons for such an apology, then certain facts must be acknowledged as part of U.S. history: that slaves and their descendants suffered grave injuries, that such injuries were a form of injustice, and that such injuries did not just happen—there were responsible parties. President Clinton's apology for the Tuskegee Study does not say that "some events in U.S. history are shameful"; it says that "what the United States did was shameful."

It is a measure of what apology extracts from apologizers that monetary compensation was offered to the Tuskegee subjects long before President Clinton's apology was proffered in 1997: Since the time the study officially ended in the early 1970s, surviving victims and their heirs had been paid at least 10 million dollars. At the time of the apology, Clinton added other financial redress in the form of seed money for a biomedical research unit at Tuskegee and some initiatives to involve minority communities in health care—something considered particularly important in light of Blacks' long-standing distrust of the health system, precisely because of experiments such as the Tuskegee Study. The apology and the financial support seem quite complementary: Money cannot substitute for the admission of inexcusable wrongdoing entailed by apology, but an apology without acknowledgment of the multiple costs of oppression and exploitation seems unknowing and insincere, especially since slavery and its attendant racism were intended in part to keep Blacks from access to all the nation's resources, including its financial ones.

If the combination of apology and reparations seems to have been welcome and appropriate in the case of something like the Tuskegee Study, wouldn't it make sense for those arguing in favor of reparations for slavery to hope for apology as well? What isn't there to like about apology?

What's worrisome about apology is that in the act of apologizing, the apologizer dons a garment with two closely woven together and not equally attractive sides: The moral virtue embodied in the sincere apology is inseparable from a kind of moral protection it provides its wearer. Let us see how this is so.

APOLOGY AND THE LOCUS OF REPAIR

James Baldwin never formally discussed apology. And he had no reason to think, in the 1960s, that an apology for slavery or racism was on the horizon. However, *The Fire*

Next Time suggests that he'd consider calls for apology to be misleading about where and how the repair work made necessary by the history of U.S. slavery and racism should occur.

Baldwin's work is a vivid reminder that "race" as it has been experienced in the United States involves heavy traffic in emotions, and much of his advice in *The Fire Next Time* is about how Blacks might carry the emotional burdens imposed by white racism, itself so sustained by and thickly striated with emotion. Though Baldwin does not explicitly bring up apology, he does mention forgiveness—but only long enough to insist that forgiving white Americans for slavery and its legacy is out of the question:

> [T]his is the crime of which I accuse my country and my countrymen, and for which neither I nor time nor history will ever forgive them, that they have destroyed and are destroying hundreds of thousands of lives and do not know it and do not want to know it.[11]

Yet, while he thereby implies that the emotional weight of resentment or anger is carriable, he clearly thinks hatred is too heavy to bear. As he sees it, the acceptable, indeed necessary, alternative to hatred is pity: After a particularly vile display of raw bigotry from whites in an airport bar, Baldwin says, "A few years ago, I would have hated these people with all my heart. Now I pitied them, pitied them in order not to despise them. And this is not the happiest way to feel toward one's countrymen" (79). Not the happiest way, but—here I begin a line of thought not developed by but encouraged to germinate on the basis of Baldwin's remarks—a way that enables one's emotions to line up with plausible lines of repair.

In ruling out forgiveness, Baldwin implies that even if the giving up of resentment necessary to forgiveness might begin to mend relations between Blacks and whites, it would be at too great a cost to Blacks. But so also, he implies, would Black hatred of whites; it wouldn't fix anything and would simply mimic white hatred of Blacks. In any event, what first needs fixing, Baldwin insists, are the souls of white folks, and in the realm of race relations, until the white psyche is rehabilitated, whites are in no position to fix anything else. However, they aren't able to fix their own souls. The only thing that can do that is the power of a fierce Black love.

The love that, according to Baldwin, whites need and Blacks are in a position to provide recognizes whites as people who don't know who they are or what they have done, people who are "bewildered and joyless and thoughtlessly cruel . . . the slightly mad victims of their own brainwashing" (137). Their pathetic investment in and obsession with white superiority reveal levels of fear and self-loathing that only love can undermine, a love which "takes off the masks [they] fear [they] cannot live without and know [they] cannot live within" (128). This is a love distinct from forgiveness; and, to return to our theme, it is a love based on a perception of whites that would be foreclosed by the logic of apology.

The repair work Baldwin describes as necessary for the white psyche cannot be accomplished by the rituals of white apology and Black forgiveness. Whites are neither the proper objects of Black forgiveness nor the proper offerers of apology to Blacks. For, on Baldwin's analysis, what is wrong with whites—the reason they require a pity-laced love from Blacks—makes it impossible for them to have the kind of understanding of the harms they have done that is a prerequisite of apology. To expect or invite an apology from them is thus to foreclose recognition of their deep lack of knowledge, itself a requisite of the real sorrow sincere apology expresses.

What, according to Baldwin, accounts for this lack of knowledge? First, and most generally, "For the horrors of the American Negro's life there has been almost no language" (95); the absence of such language threatens the availability of understanding even to those who have experienced the horrors. But even in the case of nameable and articulable horrors, "White America remains unable to believe that black America's grievances are real; they are unable to believe this because they cannot face what this fact says about themselves and their country."[12] Moreover, they have immunized themselves from the kind of criticism that might correct their misunderstandings: After all, "the white world is threatened whenever a black man refuses to accept the white world's definitions" (95). And could there be any point in Blacks looking for signs of whites' understanding of Black grievances, given Blacks' long and very bitter experience of the risks entailed in assuming "that the humanity of white people is more real to them than their color" (45)?

In addition, to the extent that one important measure

of the sincerity of an apology for injustice is the degree to which the apologizer imagines a changed world, a future in which injustice would not have to be apologized for because it would not exist, whites in their present condition seem incapable of such sincerity:

> Now, there is simply no possibility of a real change in the Negro's situation without the most radical and far-reaching changes in the American political and social structure. And it is clear that white Americans are not simply unwilling to effect these changes; they are, in the main, so slothful have they become, unable to even to envision them. (115)

In short, Baldwin's work suggests that an apology from white America for slavery and racism locates the necessary repairs at the wrong point and puts them in the hands of the wrong people. Before the would-be apologizers are in a position to do the kind of repair apology might make possible, they themselves have to be fixed, and they have shown themselves not only incapable of self-repair but unaware of their need for it. Apology, like other modes of repair, requires skills and knowledge—which in this case white Americans have been educated not to have: That's one of the ways racism works. Whites, Baldwin is urging, lack deep knowledge of the harms caused by the history of slavery and other manifestations of racism; they lack awareness of and interest in what it is about them and their institutions that has wreaked such havoc in the lives of Blacks and other nonwhites; and they have not developed the imaginative skills that would allow them to envision a world in which such horrible powers would have been tamed.

This is of course a very powerful rhetorical move by Baldwin. Denying that whites have developed the knowledge or the capacities requisite for apology, on the one hand, lets them off the hook: They are too pathetic to be blamed for what they've done. On the other hand, it makes possible a portrait of the white soul—at least in matters of "race"—as crazed, irrational, deeply doubt-ridden, their cruelty more hideous for being gratuitous, as natural as breathing.

APOLOGY AND THE SPLENDOR OF REHABILITATION

One worry about a white apology for slavery and the history of racism, then, emerging from Baldwin is that inviting or hoping for such an apology would divert both Blacks and whites from focusing on the pathological state of the white psyche. If whites are too sick to be sorry, to know what sorry could mean, they need to get well before being able to offer an apology and know what they would be saying.

Another worry about apology, however, emerges even when there is every reason to believe that the apologizer's sorrow is not only sincere but informed by a robust understanding of the grief he has caused and a recognition of the changes in him and in the larger society that would be required to put an end to such grief.

Through the vehicle of an apology, one's having been

party to evil comes wrapped in one's now being allied with good.[13] Vice is nested in virtue. The very instrument with which I acknowledge wrongdoing establishes my credentials as right-leaning, as knowing I've been off course, as already consulting the moral compass to assess and guide my behavior. The way I bring attention to the damage I've done already begins the work necessary to repair it. I don't hide my wrongdoing; I bring attention to it. I don't boast of it; I regret it. I recognize that I'm not the only occupant of the world: You count, the rules by which we live count, the fabric of our society counts.

Apology is more about the wrongdoer than it is about the wrong done and the person to whom the wrong was done. After all, there are means independent of the apology for establishing that someone has been injured; indeed, there have to be, in order to decide whether there is anything to apologize for or anything that can be apologized for (some deeds are just too morally grotesque to allow for apology). But there is no other way than apology to tell whether the person who inflicted the harm both acknowledges and regrets having done so. Apology for slavery means that slavery didn't just somehow happen. Someone, some people, made it happen, perpetuated it, benefited from it; and any apology for slavery would imply that there was no excuse for their having done so. But that someone now enters into the story of slavery cloaked in virtue, the virtue of confession, of remorse, of the hope for redemption.

So, yes, the sinner humbles herself in apologizing for her sins: She admits to wrongdoing and rules out exculpatory explanations. Apology involves, in the words of Nicholas Tavuchis, "scrupulous self-exposure to justifiable retribution"; in it "we stand naked . . . unarmed and exposed."[14] And yet in the very act of such damning self-disclosure the apologizer wraps herself in a glorious mantle of rehabilitation. However vicious her actions, however morally reprehensible she has been in the past, her sincere apology entitles her to credit at the bank of moral rectitude. She's done wrong, but she knows it, accepts full responsibility for it, and regrets it. Earlier we saw how apology forecloses a view of the apologizer as pitiably pathological. Here, we can see how it short-circuits any further criticism: The sinner has come around; her very capacity to apologize is proof positive of her already being on the road to moral recovery.

That, of course, is precisely why sincere apology is so welcoming: Once it has been offered, an acknowledgment of wrongdoing has been given, and neither the victim nor any other agents of justice need spend time rehearsing the harms that have been done or trying to pry a confession out of the wrongdoer. The repair to the victim, to the relationship between victim and wrongdoer, and to the fabric of the society has begun. It is hard to think of its being an argument against apology that the same act by which the apologizer reveals how far she's strayed from the moral path indicates that she has begun returning to it. But it's still a fact that apology does that, which suggests that once an act has been apologized for, it comes to be understood or interpreted in a different way.

Recall one of the reasons why apology seems to involve such intense exposure of the apologizer: In apologizing, he is refusing to try to hide behind exculpatory explanations of his actions, to distance himself from what he's done, or to introduce doubt about the degree of his responsibility. Apology proclaims that the very same person standing before you now regretting what he has done was fully present when he did it. He doesn't say, "Oh, I wasn't being myself," or "I couldn't help it, the devil [or the alcohol or the stress or the bad upbringing] made me do it." And yet in another sense apology does enact a distance between the apologizer and his deed: The horror of the deed seems at odds with the virtue of the apologizer now owning up fully to having committed it. Apology in this way tilts toward the revisionist.

APOLOGY AND THE CYCLES OF REPAIR

But apology does not only tend—perhaps fairly enough, but still, there it is—toward the revisionary: Could the deed have been all that dreadful if it was the deed of someone good enough to apologize? It also is diversionary, in the rather strict sense noted earlier: Once put on the table, apology switches attention to the person to whom it was offered, suggesting that the necessary repair work now devolves to the aggrieved party.

There is a sense in which apology is a self-imposed form of punishment and retaliation. For the damage I've done you, I now damage myself. In payment for your having been wronged, I acknowledge my wrongdoing; in payment for your pain of being subject to evil, I expose myself as being the perpetrator of it; in payment for your grief or fear or humiliation, I humble myself and I offer my sorrow and regret. I withdraw any implicit claim I made to the right to harm you. Apology thus has an element of eye-for-an-eye: For the pain I have brought to you, I willingly inflict pain upon myself. The unjust imbalance between us is set right by my apologizing for what I've done.

Or is it? As we saw earlier, if an apology completes one round of repairs, it initiates another: Now that I've apologized to you, what are you going to do? My apology is a kind of subpoena, pressing you for an appearance, a response. Given what I have declared, and declared openly, about my deeds and my attitude toward them, shouldn't you be pleased? Shouldn't you give up any anger and resentment you have? Don't you at least owe me some kind of response? I've owned up to what I've done, I share your sense that I was wrong, you and I are on the same page, we don't disagree. It's your beliefs about what is just and unjust that justify the anger you have felt toward me; but if I share those beliefs, I in a sense share your anger, and you have lost the moral high ground your anger might have afforded you. But more, it shifts the burden now to you. Will I, like President Clinton apologizing for the Tuskegee Study, get to thank you preemptively for "not withhold[ing] the power to forgive"?

There are, then, at least three ways which what makes apology so attractive also provide the apologizer with protective coating. Surely, it is a welcome event when one who has injured you owns up to having done so and sincerely expresses sorrow and regret for his deeds. And yet such owning up is also distracting, especially in a context of history of systematic inequality, if it keeps us from asking whether the sorrow is well informed or it forecloses inquiries into the psyche of the apologizer—the kind of inquiries that might reveal the apologizer to be other than he takes himself to be, might reveal the source of his wrongdoing to be an unflattering pathological state which would undermine his claim to superiority. Second, one cannot welcome the apologizer without welcoming the penitent, wrapped in the mantle of virtue, whose very humbleness surely should take away the sting of the harm she once wrought. The very same account of evil which tells us that it is worse to do it than to suffer it invites us to be more interested morally in the reformed apologetic evildoer than the wronged party, whose morality has not been in question. And yet now, third, the wronged party's morality does come under scrutiny: He didn't do the harm, but the kind of repair begun by the apologizer at this point requires his handiwork. He didn't do the harm, but will he pick up his share of the repair? Ah, such armor: In sorrowfully owning up to what I've done, I divert unflattering inquiries into the state of my soul, drape myself in flattering humility, and change the center of attention to you. I don't intend to do this. The ritual of apology does it for me.

REPARATIONS BRIEFLY REVISITED

Sincere but uninformed apology, we have seen, might short-circuit an attempt to spell out in sufficient detail the grievances of the injured party. Do reparations do any better job? At first glance it would seem not: Indeed, they can appear to be grotesque precisely because they try to assign a monetary value to those grievances, to echo the chorus of clueless econometricians who insist that there is nothing worth having that cannot be measured in cash terms. But suppose—as Baldwin does, for example—that the would-be apologizer does not really know the extent of the havoc he has wrought, that it is this very "innocence which constitutes the crime."[15] This is not an unreasonable supposition; racism is in part constituted by, reflected in, and sustained through the dominant group's ignorance of the ways their own lives are implicated in the grave harm done to those politically, socially, or economically subordinated to them. What are the available means of trying to drive home the nature and extent of those injustices? It may well be that were it not for the kind of "calculus of suffering"[16] reparations requires, whites would not otherwise become educated about such injustice. One reason Randall Robinson has been encouraging African Americans to push for a consideration of reparations is that he thinks it will provide a much needed incentive and avenue, even permission, for African Americans to take stock of the named and unnamed ways their individual and communal lives have been damaged by slavery and its legacy. Any such argument has even stronger force for whites. Indeed, it may well be the case that prior to the kind of inquiry that the call for reparations embodies, apology for those injuries will be premature: One has to know what one is apologizing for. So, even if reparations mean never having to say you're sorry, they may sometimes be the necessary prelude to learning just what one is sorry for.

CHAPTER 6

The Irreparable and the Irredeemable

Homo reparans stalks the land. Humans seem everywhere and ceaselessly engaged in projects of repair—nursing machines back to life, patching up friendships, devising paths of reconciliation for conflicting peoples.

But not everything that breaks can be fixed. The skills we repairing animals have to learn include the self-reflexive one of coming to grips with the limits of those skills and figuring out what to do in the face of the irreparable. In many cases the judgment that something is irreparable is not straightforward, and the declaration of irreparability represents the result of struggles over when, where, and how to use our reparative resources. Moreover, both reparability and irreparability have their consolations, so we can't assume that declarations of irreparability are always and everywhere met with dismay or disappointment.

We turn now to a variety of settings in which *H. repa-*

rans has been asked to buzz off, has been urged to recognize that the reparative skills of *Homo sapiens* are unwelcome, inadequate, or inappropriate.

RUINS AND THE RELISH OF IRREPARABILITY

Some of the most vivid scenes of the powers of decay and destruction against which under ordinary circumstances we would expect to catch *H. reparans* laboring are found in what have been called simply *ruins*. Descriptions of these cherished remains of structures or of whole cities provide a veritable inventory of disrepair: the "brute, downward-dragging, corroding, crumbling power of nature"[1] has produced "rent palaces, crushed columns,"[2] "broken towers and mouldered stones,"[3] "long-deserted cities, fallen century by century into deeper decay, their forsaken streets grown over by forest and shrubs, their decadent buildings, quarried and plundered down the years, gaping ruinous, the haunt of lizards and of owls."[4]

However, such oases of disrepair—Babylon, Palmyra, Troy, Angkor Wat, the Acropolis, Tintern Abbey, Machu Picchu, to name but a few—are in fact places where *H. reparans* is persona non grata. For unlike the state of decay, disintegration, or destruction found in familiar candidates for repair or restoration—that rusted-out 1966 Mustang, that slashed Newman painting, that broken hipbone—the state of terminal disrepair characteristic of ruins has been treated as the source of rapturous enthrallment, or at the very least, poignant instruction. The powers against which the reparative impulse works are in the case of ruins greeted without opposition and often with a passion which even has its own name: *Ruinenlust.*[5] When it comes to ruins, *H. reparans* better take off its tool belt—not so much because there is nothing it can possibly do, but because any work it might do would threaten the status of the remains as ruins and diminish their power to give pleasure or to instruct. *Pleasure of Ruins,* Rose Macaulay's inimitable romp through ruins across the world, begins with a partial list of such sweets for the eyes, thrills for the soul:

> When did it consciously begin, this delight in decayed or wrecked buildings? Very early, it seems. Since down the ages men have meditated before ruins, rhapsodized before them, mourned pleasurably over their ruination, it is interesting to speculate on the various strands in this complex enjoyment, on how much of it is admiration for the ruin as it was in its prime . . . how much is association, historical or literary, what part is played by morbid pleasure in decay, by righteous pleasure in retribution (for so often it is the proud and the bad who have fallen), by mystical pleasure in the destruction of all things mortal and the eternity of God (a common reaction in the Middle Ages), by egotistic satisfaction in surviving . . . by masochistic joy in common destruction . . . and by a dozen other entwined threads of pleasurable and melancholy emotion.[6]

Sources other than Macaulay remind us that even when pleasure is not the predominant response to ruins, they nonetheless have an irresistible draw, a potent fascination; to *Pleasure of Ruins* we must add titles such as *Fascina-*

tion of Decay and *Irresistible Decay.*[7] *Homo sapiens* has not just gone the length of the globe to see ruins, but has written about them, painted them, photographed them, woven them into fabrics, even built and inhabited sham versions of them. Over the centuries, ruins have been seen as providing instruction on many matters, including, for example, our relation to nature, to the gods, and to other human beings.

The Instructiveness of Ruins

In their palpable state of collapse, decay, and disintegration, once-grand structures wear irrefutable evidence of the overwhelming power of nature to erode, to break down, to inexorably wear away even the sturdiest of humankind's monuments. Indeed, Robert Harbison recently has reiterated a long-standing view that ruins in advanced stages of fragmentation are particularly "important not for helping us reconstruct past civilization but for assuring us there will always be something bigger than that."[8] Nature might also add insult to injury by taking up habitation in the ruins, where flora and fauna—trees, undergrowth, rodents, bats—freely exercise their squatting rights. The inevitable decay might have been hastened by past human acts of deliberate destruction (e.g., bombs or battering rams) or nature's own accelerated upheavals (e.g., volcanoes); it might have been checked at various moments by repair, restoration, or renovation; but there is no gainsaying the present state of ruination.

Recognition of nature's undeniable powers becomes

the occasion for some observers to reflect on the impermanence and transiency of everything, including human
life; and that in turn may lead some to despair (all human
endeavor is in the end futile) while providing others with
a sense of pleasurable melancholy (the beauty of things and
of people is enhanced by the necessity of their disintegration and death). Oh ruins, what dost thou tell us—that
you, and thus also we ourselves, are vanquished by nature?
or do you, and we, simply become more clearly part of it?
Is the natural world our "inevitable tomb" or our "eternal home"?[9]

To those of a particular religious sensibility, ruins are
what comes of humankind's hubris and greed. And so the
prophet Zephaniah,

> like all prophets, rejoiced over the ruin of great cities,
> confident that they had richly deserved their fate, for
> prophets have believed all large cities to be given over to
> wickedness, and an abomination in the eyes of the Lord,
> and no doubt they are right. They have been the most
> single-minded of ruin-lovers, having no use for cities un-
> til they fall, and then rejoicing over the shattered remains
> in ringing words.[10]

The twelfth-century monk Hildebert swooned before
the ruins of Rome, but did not fail to remark upon the evidence they provided of "divine chastisement."[11] Indeed,
he apparently was insistent on their not being restored or
reconstructed, for fear this message (not to mention their
matchless beauty) would be obscured. He has not been
alone in seeing ruins as underscoring the difference be-

tween imperfect, palpably mortal humans and a perfect, immortal God (though some humans have held out hope that a redemptive God will not consign them to the same fate as ruins).

If ruins speak of and speak to humans' relationship to their gods, and to nature, they also mediate our relations with other humans, both living and dead. Plato may no longer be with us, but standing in the Acropolis, the living philosopher can imagine being in conversation with him. To the inconvenient worry that Plato might not think it worth his time to bother with you, the ruins offer the reminder that finally we all come to the same end; the inevitable leveling of the constructed landscape suggests the ultimate leveling of all distinctions among humans. At the same time, ruinists may be given to think of their keen sensitivity to ruins as itself a way in which they have a leg up on others around them, those aesthetically challenged philistines who don't know the difference between ordinary decay and dilapidation, on the one hand, and pleasure-giving, instruction-imparting ruins, on the other.

Ruins and Mere Rubble

Such predictable snootiness aside, it is true that mere rubble does not a ruins make. We do not have ruins in the absence of a certain way of framing decay and disintegration. "When we frame an object as a ruin, we reclaim that object *from* its fall into decay and oblivion and *for* some kind of cultural attention and care that, in a sense, elevates its value."[12] According to Paul Zucker, Gothic cathedrals had long been *en ruine* before they became candidates for the status of ruins: During the first several decades of the eighteenth century, French and Italian artists for the most part thought of them as "barbarous and uncouth; vestiges of an architecturally degraded age in which builders were apostates from the only real civilization—that of the ancient Mediterranean world."[13] He also points out the difference between Nativity scenes depicting "shabby dilapidated-looking buildings . . . dreary edifices, which merely look as though they need the services of a carpenter" and those in which the shelter for the Holy Family is rendered as ruins.[14]

How the criteria for such distinctions are made at any given point is not our concern here, but rather simply the fact that such distinctions are drawn. For they mark the sites where the work of *H. reparans* is welcome and where it is not. Though ruins have sometimes themselves been considered candidates for repair, restoration, or reconstruction, the literature on ruins is filled with lamentation over such attempts at intervention. The renowned nineteenth-century art critic John Ruskin has not been alone in thinking that to restore is to destroy; Rose Macaulay joins other ruinists in judging that central to the appreciation of ruins is "the apprehension felt . . . that weather and vegetation would in time totally disintegrate the ruins, dragging them down to moulder in the damp earth until they become one with it."[15] She recognizes why some may feel "that old Goa should be taken in hand by archaeologists, its decay arrested before it entirely crumbles away, that buildings should be restored and roads defined before all traces are forest-drowned, that it should become a celebrated goal for travellers," though she seems to side with those who think that "this would be, as nearly always, to rub the bloom from a fruit in exquisite decay, and that Velha Goa thus taken in hand would lose the peculiar rotten-ripe flavour that now enspells its phantom streets."[16] Or, as Michael Roth more recently has put it: "The balance that makes an object a ruin is destroyed when the edifice is saved."[17] So, the ruins may not be beyond repair, but extensive repair would destroy their desired brokenness.

Worries about Ruinenlust

The unbridled enthusiasms of ruinists have themselves been the subject of considerable reflection. On the one hand, ruins lovers have been mildly ridiculed as harmless eccentrics. Macaulay cites John Earle's 1628 commentary on the passions and habits of antiquaries:

> He is a man strangely thrifty of time past. . . . He is one that hath that unnatural disease to be enamoured of old age and wrinkles, and loves all things (as Dutchman do cheese) the better for being mouldy and worm-eaten . . . a broken statue would almost make him an idolater. A great admirer he is of the rust of old monuments, and reads only those characters where time hath eaten out the letters. He will go you forty miles to see a saint's well or a ruined abbey. . . . Printed books he condemns, as a novelty of this latter age, but a manuscript he pores on ever-

lastingly, especially if the cover be all moth-eaten. . . .
His grave does not fright him, for he has been used to
sepulchres, and he likes death the better because it gath-
ers him to his fathers.[18]

Eccentric behavior is one thing; acts of desecration are
another. In the eyes of at least some contemporary American Indians, the ruins of ancient tribal communities are
not places where ancestors used to live but where their
spirits still reside; moreover, restorations of kivas and other
buildings are at odds with the natural return of wood and
clay—for that matter, everything and all of us—to the
earth. The tension between the institutionalization of
Ruinenlust and the cultural practices of people whose ancestors inhabited/inhabit ruins is sometimes embodied in
the persons of Park Service employees. A young Navajo
Park Service ranger whose job it is to show tourists around
the Betatakin Ruin in Arizona is not fully at ease in her
new surroundings: "My grandmother didn't want me to
take this job. She said, 'You shouldn't go near those places.
They should be left alone. You shouldn't be there. You
shouldn't be taking people there.'"[19] It can hardly be a
source of relief to the young woman's grandmother to
learn that at such sites tourists are reminded that the ruins
through which they are about to roam are held sacred, or
to read that Native Americans have been involved in ruins
stabilization projects,[20] if the very project of preserving
the ruins and the presence of outsiders constitute violations of her and other people's deeply held beliefs and
practices. In any event, it is clear that significant cultural
differences may come to light in conflicts between Indian

and non-Indian peoples over the very meaning of ruins and the proper way to treat them. Such tension shows up visually at the Aztec Ruins in northwest New Mexico: One site, the west ruins, includes a thoroughly restored kiva, and workers often are on the scene shoring up crumbling walls and trying to keep plant life and water from undermining their structural integrity; the other site, the east ruins, is more or less being left alone.

Yet another concern about the passion for ruins is that an overly refined appreciation for decay, dilapidation, and dereliction makes one insensitive to the kind of violence that may have created them: "It is one thing to aestheticize the gradual decay of monumental buildings, another to aestheticize the effects of disaster."[21] Ruins can reflect and embody the history of the horrors of human conflict, testify to the capacity of some humans to harness the forces of nature in order to drive out or decimate others; and *Ruinenlust* at least sometimes threatens to obscure or trivialize such hard facts. In a photograph taken in 1922, Albert Einstein stands in front of some French rubble left in the wake of World War I; he regarded such ruination, at that moment, not as a source of pleasure or fascination, but as a wretchedly palpable reminder of the horrible destructiveness of war.[22] Rose Macaulay, who loved both observing ruins and recounting the manifold pleasures others found in them, carefully and with obvious deep sadness inventoried the manifold damage to body and soul wrought by war.[23]

Still, is it possible to delight in the rubble of destruction and yet not be favorably awed by the human activity that produced it? "How distant in time need [ruins] be for us to *enjoy* them and to discuss this enjoyment in public?"[24] The concern animating these questions is simply heightened by the oft-voiced suggestion on the part of many ruinists that the building or the city is even more beautiful in its ruined state than it ever was when in prime or peak condition, that "in this half-ruined grandeur" there is "a magnificence nobler than its original form," something "*plus beau que la beaute.*"[25]

Many of these questions about ruins have arisen with particular poignancy and urgency in deliberations over what to do with the rubble of the World Trade Center. According to Herbert Muschamp, the architecture critic for the *New York Times,* "We will probably see no more eloquent reminder of that day [September 11, 2001] than the twisted steel walls that at present rise from the wreckage of the World Trade Center."[26] Though he himself is not in favor of preserving "The Walls" forever, he pleads that they "not be treated as junk"—a view that he fears may have been animating the police in their scuffle with firefighters over the disposition of the wreckage. "The conflict was as much over meaning as it was over access. The police represented the view that the wreckage is now cartage. To the firefighters, it is sacred space, at least until they have fulfilled their duty to recover the victims' remains." Muschamp is acutely aware of the dangers in aestheticizing the terrible evidence of terrible deeds, but he insists, "If you believe that beauty begins in terror, then it is not sacrilege to speak of the beauty of the remaining walls." He then goes on to urge not only those who will have the responsibility for figuring out what to do with the site, but all "those now gazing on ground zero" to study ruinists such as Piranesi, the eighteenth-century artist and architect so important to the cultivation of *Ruinenlust* (and in fact the *Times* article has at its center Piranesi's "Temple of Isis at Pompeii").

Ruins are not just any state of disrepair. And it's a good bet that *Ruinenlust* tours don't include sites of urban blight, what Dolores Hayden has summarized as the "polluted harbors, abandoned housing units, rusting bridges, broken water mains" of inner cities[27]—though Robert Harbison has suggested that a latter-day Piranesi would be found taking the train from New York to Philadelphia, through the backyards of postindustrial America, gaping in awe at abandoned factories and warehouses.[28] Nor, we can pretty well be sure, do ruinists relish the thought of getting to their far-flung destinations via dilapidated airplanes or leaky boats, wearing torn clothing and drying their bodies with ancient moth-eaten towels. There is a difference between a state of disrepair to which one eagerly rushes and a state of disrepair from which one desperately flees.[29]

THE IRREDEEMABILITY OF ATROCITY

Part of the evidence for the ubiquity of humanity's repair projects is the wide variety of resistance to such endeavors. Ruinists are one example. Another variation on such resistance comes from a quite different quarter, among those troubled by what they take to be a rush to find signs of salvation and redemption in the testimonies of Holocaust survivors.

Lawrence Langer, among others, finds the language of repair widespread in interpretations of those accounts. In books such as *Holocaust Testimonies: The Ruins of Memory*[30] and *Pre-empting the Holocaust,*[31] he has done much to locate and try to undermine what he takes to be its inappropriately redemptive logic. The experiences of Holocaust survivors, he worries, have been preempted by what we have been treating here as the reparative impulse, which Langer finds not in the oral testimonies of the survivors themselves, but in the eagerness of many interviewers and interpreters to find reparative motifs.[32] Indeed, paradoxically, the lessons about repair and restoration that, according to Langer, have inappropriately been wrung out of survivor accounts are not unlike those extracted by ruinists from their beloved sites of disrepair: Just as the grandeur of a past civilization is evident in and its beauties enhanced by their current condition of fragment and decay, so, the redemptive logic goes, the resiliency of the human spirit shines even more brightly in its having held firm against the horrible forces brought to bear upon it. Just as the deterioration suffered by human monuments offers all manner of redeeming reflections for those willing to see it as something other than mere decay, so the suffering of human beings under the weight of unbearable evil offers a host of useful insights for those eager to ignore or deny the possibility of meaningless pain: Suffering ennobles the sufferer and edifies the observer; it doesn't have to kill you and is not so disabling that you cannot recover from it, find compensation for it, restore the rhythm of your life despite the full stop it came to.

It seems apt even if paradoxical to compare the ruinist enthusiasm for decay and deterioration to the bright rhetoric of redemption and salvation that Langer finds characteristic of much commentary on survivor testimony. Apt because each finds gold in the dross of brokenness and disrepair; but paradoxical because, while *Ruinenlust* seems to be about the consolations of disrepair, preemptive Holocaust readings offer the consolations of repair. As is underscored in the subtitle of *Holocaust Testimonies: The Ruins of Memory,* Langer relies on the concept of ruins to provide what he hopes is the necessary counterweight to the rhetoric of repair, redemption, and salvation.

To treat oral testimonies of survivors as anything other than a form of ruins, Langer implies, amounts to a kind of denial—not a denial of the fact or the long reach of the Holocaust, but a denial of the irreparable brokenness it caused to those who endured it. " 'You're not supposed to see this; it doesn't go with life. It doesn't go with life. These people come back, and you realize, they're all broken. Broken. Broken.' "[33]

Survivors' memories are ruin and rubble. They are the chaotic tumbling together of unspeakably violent shattering of body, soul, and community; the unforgiving jumble of death and destruction; the unmendable disruption of life, of connection with others, of a self with familiar moral contours; the end of hope, of faith, even of predictability of human behavior, whether one's own or one's tormentors and torturers. There is nothing in such ruins one can repair, restore, redeem, salvage, be compensated for, recover from, reconcile with the rest of one's life. There is nothing out of which renewal is possible: no rebuilding, no reconstructing, no healing. Langer's reading of the oral testimonies of survivors leads him to conclude that for them "nothing exists to redeem the moment they recall, and to their dismay, nothing exists to redeem them as they recall it."[34]

These ruins are nothing like the cherished objects of those stricken with *Ruinenlust:* There is no pleasure or even the thin gruel of instruction in these ruins of memory, which continue to be the source of anguish over the inability to recover what one has lost, of humiliation over the sense of confusion and incompetence the memories reignite. Part of the frisson of pleasure architectural ruins give visitors comes from the palpable sense of the buildings or fragments decaying before one's very eyes: The deterioration is not something that is over or that has been sealed up; one witnesses it directly. However, Langer insists, the ruins that are survivors' memories are still-festering injuries, not yet and not likely to be sealed by healing scar tissue: "A scar is a reminder of a curable condition, a past injury healed in the present. What we are really speaking of . . . is a festering wound, a blighted convalescence."[35] What's worrisome to many ruinists is that schemes of repair and restoration might in fact work: that the next time one returns to a favorite haunt, instead of finding it in an ever more ripe state of ruin, one will observe it as it more or less was some hundred or two hundred or thousand years ago; it will have been restored to that earlier state, a whole chunk of its history lopped off, an earlier condition renewed. What we learn from the ruins of survivors' memories, Langer urges, is precisely the opposite: that there is no such restoration possible, no selective erasure of that part of one's past: "Humiliated memory is an especially intense form of uncompensating recall. Instead of restoring a sense of power or control over a disabling past (one of the presumed goals of therapy—and perhaps of history too), it achieves the reverse, reanimating the governing impotence of the worst moments in a distinctly non-therapeutic way." Survivors "sabotage the illusion of continuity" fished for by interviewers asking whether "in your life afterwards have you rebuilt some of the things that you have lost"; memories are "monument[s] to ruins rather than reconstruction" or "restoration."[36] In the work of Primo Levi and others, "survival did not mean a restored connection with what had gone before."[37] That is, there is a sense in which survivors' memories are even more tenacious and resilient than ruins, whose worshippers worry, on the one, hand that they will be wrecked by restorative efforts but, on the other, that without such efforts they finally will disappear: Such memories do not disappear, cannot be forgotten or repressed, and make it impossible to return to, be restored to, one's earlier life.

These ruins of memory cannot be razed, but neither can the lives of which they are a part be restored to an earlier moment. Those with such memories do continue to live—indeed, to live both normally and successfully by many criteria: They have families, they maintain good jobs, they move about with relative ease in their communities. What then is the relation of that rubble of memory to their lives? What Langer has to say about this suggests that there is an analogy, albeit a limited one, between the manner in which such memories are incorporated into the rest of survivors' lives and the way Lebbeus Woods conceives of the place of the rubble of war in the architecture of Sarajevo.[38] Woods's designs incorporate the ruins of battle into new buildings in such a way as to suggest that the past is not to be forgotten and yet also not to be definitive. Like such rubble, survivors' memories provide neither the foundation for their lives ("one goes on living in spite of the toxin")[39] nor something that is neatly reconciled with, seamlessly integrated into the rest of their lives. The rubble is just there, not razable, not redeemable, not pretty. Unlike the architecture of buildings, however, the architecture of memory is not a matter of choice; survivors do not choose to include those experiences in the bank of their memories, nor, if Langer is right, is it appropriate to think of them as providing lessons about healing, or "the human condition," or "man's fate" for the rest of humankind. "The unappeasable experience is part of [survivors'] inner reality, and though the optimistic American temperament winces at the notion," survivors know that what they have "survived is an event to be endured, not a trauma to be healed."[40]

The experience of the Holocaust, Langer holds, not only left untreatable, irredeemable wounds in those who were not murdered. It also ripped into "the fundamental integrity of the social and religious fabric of which Western culture is woven."[41] We get a sense of the fabric he has in mind and also of his worries about redemptive misreadings of the rents to it in his remarks on Viktor Frankl's *Man's Search for Meaning* (which Langer suggests is "perhaps more widely read than any other book on the concentration camp experience"):

> It is as if Frankl approached the crumbling edifice of twentieth-century humanism in Auschwitz armed with intellectual and moral props from an earlier era. He is determined to shore up the ruins and to reassure his readers that in fact there has been no irreparable damage to the architecture of thought about the human spirit from Spinoza and Lessing to Nietzsche and Rilke, and up to the present. He cites all of these, in addition to Dostoevsky, Tolstoy, Schopenhauer, Bismarck, and Thomas Mann (together with Ecclesiastes and the Gospel of John). And they *do* reassure. It is comforting to hear from Frankl that Dostoevsky once said: "There is only one thing that I dread: not to be worthy of my sufferings." It is even more consoling to hear Nietzsche's aphorism: *"Was mich nicht umbringt, macht mich staerker"* ("That which does not kill me makes me stronger.") But such a system of allusion and analogy causes our experience of Auschwitz to be filtered through the purifying vocabulary of an earlier time. The wary reader, though perhaps comforted and consoled by such a system, will understand the verbal assertion that has been imposed on a chaotic reality in order to reweld an apparently broken connection between Auschwitz and the literary-philosophical traditions nurturing Frankl's vision.[42]

If there is any lesson to be learned, any wisdom to be gained from the experience of survivors, it is not about the promise of healing, the possibility of redemption, the path of rebuilding, but the necessity of rethinking what we mean by "civilization," of considering whether the forces of inhumanity aren't more powerful than the impulses to humanity. Until we better understand the atrocities that blight the human landscape, we'll not be in a position to come to the aid of their victims. We "must begin by acknowledging that the usual consolations may not apply, that efforts to heal by forgetting the past and bravely facing the future might only betray a misunderstanding of the effects of atrocity on the human body, mind, and spirit."[43] Langer is not denying anyone the need or the right to try to understand the effects of the Holocaust on its victims. But he is eager to make sure that we don't assume that such understanding will be consolatory.

Langer's is just one among many voices in the ongoing project of providing an adequate or at least not horribly misleading understanding of those effects. For students of the presence and scope of the reparative impulse in human affairs—as it is expressed not only in our activities but in our interpretations of those activities—Langer's work on Holocaust testimonies is an urgent and sustained plea to bracket off the rich and varied language of repair in attempts to provide some kind of meaning, some measure of intelligibility to survivors' accounts of what they endured then and still experience so many years later. "The urgency to undo ruin has always outpaced the desire to confront it."[44] Aware as he is of the very generous inventory of repair words, Langer is eager to make sure none of them gets to slip unchecked into the conversation. The promise of reparability is introduced only to be cancelled in the same breath by the bluntness of irreparability: A survivor's memories "create a break in the chain of her life that telling cannot mend"; "humiliated memory thus forces us into an unnatural relation with the past, because the 'knowledge' it imparts crushes the spirit and frustrates the incentive to renewal"; memory becomes "a monument to ruin rather than reconstruction."[45] "As for renewal or rebirth, such monuments to hope cannot be built from the ruins of a memory crammed with images of flame and ash."[46] Of the paintings of Samuel Bak, Langer says: "His metaphors demand that we re-view, and then review, well-known models of spiritual consolation and consider how they may have been recast by secular ruin."[47]

In short, the constellation of repair words are laid out before us in order for us to be warned off of their use: renewal, redemption, reconciliation, salvation, compensation, consolation, resiliency, restoration, repair; to heal, mend, recover, rebuild, resolve, reconstruct. In their stead we should be ready to recognize the appropriateness of the family of disrepair words and phrases: to break, rupture, rent, crush, ruin; damage and loss that is irreversible, irreplaceable, unredeemed, irredeemable, irreparable; states of being that are unmendable, untreatable, unsalvageable, unreconcilable. Indeed, Langer thinks that it is only when we are deprived of the consoling hopefulness of the language of repair that we might be motivated "to intercede in situations of atrocity before they have spent their energy, leaving negotiated 'reconciliation' as the only practical course of action."[48]

Langer thus inadvertently makes in a most startling way a point at the center of this larger exploration: that repair is ubiquitous and various; that the language of repair is always there for the taking; and that judgments about what can be repaired and what can't, what should be repaired and what shouldn't—indeed, whether the language of repair may in fact disincline us to think about prevention —guide the deployment and distribution of some of our most precious resources.

For example, let's for the moment juxtapose the widespread presumption of irreparability in the case of inmates in U.S. prisons with the presumption of reparability in the case of Holocaust survivors. There is considerable agreement that at this point in the history of the U.S. criminal justice system, prisoners are treated for all intents and purposes as being in a state of terminal disrepair, as being either not capable of or not worth the trouble of rehabilitation. In fact, that has been so much the consensus among prison observers that the *New York Times* considered it front-page material in May 2001 to report that rehabilitative efforts have perhaps begun to make a small return.[49] Though prisons have been described variously as penitentiaries, reformatories, houses of correction, sites of rehabilitation, the much more recent reference to them as warehouses signals the loss of even the pretense of their providing some kind of rehabilitative services. *H. reparans,* once apparently a welcome visitor in so many of the earlier incarnations of the prison, has been stopped at the gate. Perhaps being considered hopelessly in disrepair has come to be thought of as an appropriate punishment for one's deeds. Or, given the hugely disproportionate percentage of Black and Latino men and women in U.S. prisons— in 1999, Blacks constituted 46 percent, Latinos, 16 percent of the prison population[50]—perhaps it is yet another reminder of one's relative place in the larger society.

If, in the case of prisoners, reparability has been preempted, the consolations of irreparability can set in: No one—government officials, wardens, guards, the rest of the citizenry—need worry about efforts to rehabilitate inmates if doing so is either impossible or not worth the effort and money. Some people, on this view, are just too evil to be fixable.

And if, in the case of Holocaust testimonies, irreparability has been preempted, room can open up for the consolations of reparability: The testimonies of Holocaust survivors could then be seen as affirming that no matter how savagely, cruelly, inhumanly people are treated, there is something they can redeem from their experiences, always some way to rebuild their lives, to recover from brokenness. The forces of evil, on this view, cannot do irreparable harm.

But sometimes they can.

CHAPTER 7

Repair, the Old, and the New

Repair is conservative: It makes it possible for what has existed in the past to continue into and beyond the present. Repair gets the car running again, the friendship back on its legs, the community able to resume civil functioning. But in order to bring about this link to the past, in order to undo the damage, repair has to do something about those breakdowns, ruptures, and collapses. In this sense, repair is interventionist, a characteristic that family members implicitly note when they wonder whether they ought to let the surgeons try one more repair or simply leave their loved one to "die a natural death." Curators of historical buildings have been taught by authorities in the field to think of options before them in terms of degrees of intervention: "We can ... classify levels of intervention according to a scale of increasing radicality, thus: (1) preservation; (2) restoration; (3) conservation and consolidation; (4) reconstitution; (5) adaptive reuse; (6) reconstruction; (7) replication."[1]

In bowing deeply toward the past, allowing a previous condition to dictate what needs to be done, repair requires the kind of humility that, according to Lewis Mumford, is a hard-earned achievement of *H. sapiens:*

> In dealing with the forces of nature, man's animism got him nowhere. He might attribute willful mischief to a pot that leaked or to a basket that came apart when it was filled . . . but he could not come to terms with these recalcitrant objects by any amount of sympathetic communication. Eventually, he would have to overcome his anger or indignation sufficiently to patch the leak or reweave the badly woven osier, if he wants to make it perform its function. That humility before the object, that respect for function, were essential both to man's intellectual and his emotional development.[2]

And yet repair is also presumptuous in its insistence that a given point in the history of something, or a given condition of something, is more important than any other point or condition; for while repair in one sense honors the past by paying homage to an earlier moment, in another sense it erases the past by undoing much of what in the meantime has happened. Hence the conflicts, for example, between preservers of historical sites and those who would repair and restore them over what moment of history ought to be the community's focus: Should the crumbling gas chambers at Birkenau "be restored, somewhat restored or be allowed to fade into oblivion"?[3]

To repair, then, is to enact a complicated attitude toward the past and the preexistent: Repair is conservative, but also interventionist; humble, but also presumptuous; it honors some moments in the past while erasing others. In its service to the past and the preexistent we find reasons to distinguish repairing something from creating it or replacing it, and in the conservative commitment of repair to continuity we note its difference from destruction.

This profile of repair suggests that human beings, like the rest of the natural world of which we are part, exhibit at least three kinds of impulses, embody at least three kinds of forces, which we can observe in our ability to create, to destroy, and to repair.

The task of repairing something is often defined, implicitly or explicitly, in contrast to creating it. Recall Willie's own understanding of his work as in large part dictated by "the engineer who built [the cars] in the first place," whose design Willie imagines as he thinks about the best way to attack the problem before him.[4] At the same time, absence of constraints upon his redesigning efforts marked his work as different from that of Elisabeth, Louise, and Irene: Willie often went on to think of himself as replacing, not just following, the original engineer, but the distinction between Barnett Newman as creator of *Cathedra* and Elisabeth, Louise, and Irene as restorers was not to be crossed. The fact that Irene and her associates might all too easily cross that boundary does not mean that because they are excellent restorers of works of art they also are good creators of art. Their knowledge of how to restore *Cathedra* no more automatically translates into their being capable of creating a *Cathedra* than it translates into their being capable of repairing the cars in Willie's garage. And artists themselves on the whole do not know how to restore their own works (as opposed to, say, painting over them).

So, it seems that part of our coming to understand the nature of repair, to see just what it is dear *H. reparans* does, is recognizing ways in which it is distinct from creation. Repair is about trying to preserve some kind of continuity with the past, with objects or relationships that already exist and have fallen prey to damage or decay. Creation is the process by which those things come into existence to begin with. It's perhaps not surprising that the distinction between creation and repair becomes particularly sharp in certain religious contexts: The influence on some nineteenth-century surgeons of John Dryden's sentiment that "God did not make his Works for man to mend"[5] is echoed in a concern voiced at the end of the twentieth century by some bioethicists over certain advances in medicine: "If you get in there with your wrenches and screwdrivers, you're violating God's creation."[6] But you don't need to be religious to have the distinction between creation and repair brought to your attention. It seems straightforward: There are people or beings or processes by which or through which things are created, come into existence. Those things are bound to decay or break or disintegrate. The range of activities we broadly call repair returns these already existing things to an earlier state. There wouldn't be restorers of works of art if there weren't works of art. You can't mend a friendship if it doesn't exist. You can't restore a country to democracy if it never enjoyed democracy to begin with.

So much perhaps seems clear—but only if we refuse to

notice all the deep fissures in the walls alleged to separate creation from repair. For one thing, a lot of repair work requires a great deal of creativity if it is to be successful. It's not only because Willie's customers are short on cash and because, by dint of necessity, he is a *bricoleur* that he is constantly called upon to "redefine the fixability of objects."[7] It's also because, as he puts it, " 'Things are broken or worn in different ways—they each have their own characteristics,' "[8] and if he's going to do even a decent repair job, he can't always turn to a manual or his own early precedents for a ready-made solution. True, many of his tasks might have been made easier if he'd had available to him the option of replacing whole modules or units of cars to deal with problems or defects in some smaller part. But not only has this practice tended to raise the cost of repairs (to the point where some insurance companies are pressing car manufacturers to cease such practices); latter-day versions of Willie, such as Honda/Acura specialist Bob Abrams, rue the ways the creativity of their work is being eroded by the use of such wholesale replacement.[9] Advocates of restorative justice celebrate the creative, very context-sensitive solutions victims, offenders, and community representatives come up with in response to crime and other conflict—indeed, it's precisely such creativity that concerns critics of the movement, who worry that such keen case-specific thinking is bound to undermine the aspirations to fairness and proportionality across cases that justice requires. So, even if good repairers do not exercise creativity by bringing new things into existence, they are by the very nature of their work called upon to exercise creativity in keeping things from going out of existence or in putting broken connections among humans back together.

But the fractures in the wall sustaining the distinction between creation and repair don't just come from the creativity of repair. They also are due to the reparative and revisionary nature of creation. A certain view of the nature of creation has held sway off and on for centuries, at least in many Western cultures, according to which creators of paintings or poems or theories are delivered of their creations fully and more or less all at once. It may take a bit of time to get it all out—let's see, the Creator took six days, and even little Mozart had to labor long enough to deliver the whole composition—but the object emerges from the creative womb fully formed. On this view, works of creative genius no more need repair than the world as God created it did—and to suggest otherwise is as much a misunderstanding of and insult to human creators as it would be in the case of the divine one. Perfect things don't need fixing. If they did, they wouldn't be perfect.

It may seem as if spelling out such a view is enough to condemn it, or at least limit its applicability to a very small selection of the works of a very small number of people. But such a view about creativity continues to exert a powerful influence. The poet W. H. Auden's literary executor, Edward Mendelson, has written about the scolding Auden got for presuming to publish revised versions of his poetry, as if he were ruining his own creation and giving the lie to cherished notions of genius and creativity—or as if Auden were violating his own work in the way Elisabeth, Louise, and Irene would be violating Newman's *Cathedra* were they to make changes in it. Auden's critics seemed unwilling to countenance a view about the construction of poems according to which "the work is never entirely finished, because the author continually finds weak links that need repairs or improvements."[10] More recently, there has been quite a lot of public reflection by writers, dancers, and other artists on the critical role of revision and repair in their work—which wouldn't be necessary, or seem worth revealing and exploring, if they weren't implicitly reacting to the still powerful notion that creators are not repairers.[11]

So, if we want to find where the work of repair fits in among all the other things humans do, calling on a distinction between repair and creation isn't a bad place to begin. But it's not a distinction to grab onto too tightly, for it tends to obscure the creativity that much repair requires and the repairs and revisions that most creation entails.

Perhaps repair is more distinct from destruction than it is from creation. After all, what intentional or unintentional destruction accomplishes is the end of something, its demise, its irreparability. If repair is about trying to preserve some kind of continuity with the past, keeping some aspect of it alive, destruction is about producing discontinuity with the past, trying to make sure the past is past, that it's over and done with. The World Trade Center's twin towers are beyond repair. Willie is admired for his ability to "make it possible for Saabs in the area to carry on for ten, fifteen, even twenty years"[12]—to keep them from the wrecker's ball, the jaws of the scrap-yard crusher. That the reparative impulse in human beings works against the destructive forces of nature is precisely why *H. reparans* is persona non grata at the site of beloved ruins. According to Lawrence Langer, those who misread the testimonies of Holocaust survivors fail to see that the horrible destructive powers of some humans against others sometimes are so overwhelming that they make acting on the reparative impulse out of the question. When a part of you has been shattered and destroyed, there is no rescue or repair effort that can restore it.

All these observations and claims turn on a distinction between the reparative impulse in humans and the destructive impulse in humans or in nature. But here, too, the distinction is tidier than the phenomena it is meant to reflect. Repair is hedged round with anxiety that the very process by which something is repaired will destroy it. The point here is not that the repair might go awry—that the hammer might slip, the scalpel fall, the paint remover spill, the apology be undermined by the blatant attempt to excuse one's behavior. The distinction between repair and destruction gets smudged when the worry is that a successful repair project destroys the very thing so well mended. Sometimes this is because, while the repair job is excellent, it is of the wrong kind. Here's an example from William Streeter: The bookbinder may do a bang-up job restoring the family Bible to look the way it did when Great-grandmother bought it, but he ignored the customer's request to simply do enough repairs to make it possible to use the book. The imprint of Great-grandmother's hands is now gone, as is almost all other evidence of family members' use over the generations.[13] As James Marston Fitch and other experts on the historical preservation of buildings have pointed out, the distinction between preservation and restoration is not simply a casual matter of word choice, but marks the difference between "maintenance of the artifact in the same physical condition as when it was received by the curatorial agency" and "the process of returning the artifact to the physical condition in which it would have been at some previous state of its . . . development." It's precisely because past restoration practices brought about irreversible changes in objects— effectively destroying them—that, as Fitch puts it, "reversibility is a criterion which has developed from a century's experience in archaeology and art conservation."[14] Jean Améry worried that the "natural" process through which time might heal the wounds inflicted on him by the Nazis and their collaborators would destroy what was left of his own moral compass, erode the passion with which he demanded a full acknowledgment of and accounting for the atrocities sanctioned by and too hastily buried by the German people. He sought out a means of repair that would not in his eyes be morally compromising.

But sometimes no kind of repair is appropriate precisely because the successful repair of *any* kind would destroy the object in question. Whenever a state of brokenness is found more desirable than wholeness, repair doesn't destroy the object itself, of course, but it does destroy the desired state of the object. To the old saw "If it ain't broke, don't fix it" we sometimes must add: "Don't fix it even if it is broke." If the story of which we are reminded by the shattered vase is better told by the vase in shards than the vase visibly or invisibly mended, then its repair would in effect destroy the object in its prized state. Even if, as we learn from the Japanese aesthetic referred to as *wabi,* visibly repaired teapots can be more beautiful than unbroken ones, the creation of such beauty through repair might destroy the power of the still broken object to carry memory. Though visible repairs can be vehicles of memory, objects left broken sometimes are better repositories of memory than visibly repaired ones.

Paradoxically, the inherent destructiveness of repair is crucial to its capacity to console us about the passage of time and the inevitability of breakage, decay, and damage. Things have been a certain way—the car has been running, the friendship has been going along just fine, the nations have been free of conflict—but now have broken down. The prospect of repair offers the consolation that we can be reunited with that moment in the past before the break occurred. But how is destruction crucial to such consolation?

We call upon the *Homo reparans* in ourselves or in others if we wish to, as we say, pick up the threads of the past. But that means we have to destroy the state of brokenness, a state that is as much a part of the history of the car or the friendship or the political relationship as any other state. The difference between visible mending and invisible mending—between the palpably fixed teapot and the apparently never torn jacket—is the difference between revealing and hiding such history, between exposing and burying the evidence that there was a state of brokenness.

Ruinists worry that the state of brokenness that gives them such a rush of pleasure will be destroyed by repair or restoration.

Repair destroys brokenness. The consolation it offers is that undesirable states of brokenness can themselves be broken. For states of disrepair are as subject to destruction as are states of repair. If someone puts back together the vase I have left broken since the day my dying mother dropped it, I can try to repair what they've done by disassembling it once again, returning it to its broken state. But their repair likely as not destroyed the state of the vase I cherished (indeed, if it's true, as Willie says, that no two things are broken in the same way, perhaps it also is true that no one thing is broken in the same way twice). I'd have wanted the vase repaired only if I hadn't liked or valued its being broken. When I offer an apology to you for my thoughtlessness, I am seeking to destroy the state of rupture between us. The consolation apology offers depends on its capacity to be destructive in this way.

Repair is the creative destruction of brokenness. A Rose Macaulay worries that ingenious repairers will destroy the brokenness she loves; a Lawrence Langer is at pains to point out that there are some states of brokenness that even the most ingenious of repairers and restorers cannot undo. Irreparability is a state of brokenness that cannot be destroyed. Reparability is a state of brokenness that can.

While there are books and institutions that celebrate and study invention and inventors, we don't seem to have carved out similar conceptual and physical space for celebrating and studying repair and repairers. Museums—at least in the West—exist in part to celebrate creativity. There is a small cottage industry of books about the creative impulse in humans—about what it is, how to bring it out in oneself or one's young charges, the qualities of societies, such as fifteenth-century Florence, that seem to nourish it.[15] The woeful tales of humankind's destructive powers are ready at hand in accounts of war, genocide, and other atrocities.

And yet, given our reliance on repair and the skills of mind, hand, or heart it can require—sometimes in exquisite combination—there has been an astonishing lack of attention to the nature of repair, the kinds of capacities it engages, and the nature of the activities it involves. It's not that we don't talk about it—this book is chock full of examples of the way we think about it, talk about it, laugh or cry over it. But we don't seem to highlight it: In our reflections on what humanity is capable of or what humanity is up to, repairing doesn't seem to be worth noting, as if it somehow is not in the same class as other well-known human activities.

There is the occasional feature story about ingenious repairers—for example, specialists in the repair of broken toys. Their skills are particularly appreciated at toy fairs, during which, a toy company executive gushed, "The technicians who make it all work are the unsung heroes."[16] But repair seems to lack the drama and the splash associated with creation and destruction, those other powerful forms of intervention in the world with which, as we have seen, repair typically is contrasted. Repairers don't seem to be cast either in the image of godlike creators, with capacities to bring things into existence ex nihilo, or godlike destroyers, with powers to take things out of existence ad nihilum.

In any event, repair is necessary because—theological views aside—we are manifestly imperfect creatures in an imperfect world. We are reminded of this any time something or somebody or some relationship needs fixing. You can't bring up repair without thereby bringing up all manner of facts about humans and the world we inhabit that perhaps for the most part we just don't like being reminded of—that we are damaged goods, that we live in a world of damaged goods. Repairers deal with the used objects of the world, with those things bearing evidence of the trajectory toward destruction and termination. As repairers, they undertake to halt the march toward extinction, but their very existence reminds us that such extinction is inevitable.

Furthermore, the property in objects of being reparable and the capacity in people to repair things cannot be highly valued in any society whose economy is based on the production of new objects and thus depends on creating and sustaining the desire for the new. Repair is at odds with the imperatives of a capitalist consumer economy except where the repairer needs new supplies to do her work or where new products or new services such as magazines, Web sites, or referral agencies can piggyback on the work of repair.

People who are satisfied, even happy, with an object

that is well made and for which repairs are neither frequent nor expensive are not good citizens of a capitalist economy dependent upon the production and consumption of new articles. This point is vividly made in the English film *The Man in the White Suit,* in which a determined inventor discovers a recipe for a fabric that never gets dirty and lasts forever. Our hero's invention is welcomed by neither the captains of industry nor the many workers whose livelihood depends upon the reiteration of the need for new clothing. Indeed, it is hard to tell whether capitalism created or simply is delighted to take advantage of the social stigma attached to making do by fixing and mending.

Repair is not about the new. It is by definition about the survival of the old. Repair appears to be not about making progress but about halting decay, about sustaining something after it has degenerated from its ideal state. Inventive as repair can be, it is not about creating original objects or even about keeping existing objects from breaking (that is maintenance), but about responding to the damage they have endured and finding a way to continue their existence in the aftermath of such damage.

In devising such paths of continuity, repair appears to be neither a science nor an art—another reason, perhaps, for its not being on the radar screen of significant human doings. Though many forms of repair draw on knowledge gained through science—Elisabeth, Louise, and Irene, for example, couldn't properly restore the artworks left in their care without knowing about the chemical and optical properties of paint; the training of surgeons includes studies in biochemistry, physiology, and so forth—being a good scientist does not mean one will necessarily be a good repairer. And, of course, in many cases of repair there just isn't a scientific background to draw upon—there is no such thing as a science of apology or a science of reconciliation. Repair in its many forms probably comes closer to being an art rather than a science (if we have to choose between the two), but even then, repair has been seen as the handmaiden to art, derivative upon that which already exists.

Perhaps then it is not surprising that there doesn't seem to have been much interest historically in reflecting at length on the nature of repair. It appears not to have the pizzazz of creation or destruction. To think about repair requires us to recognize our own failures and imperfections and those of the world we live in, to take seriously what we may unreflectively be inclined to regard as the necessary but uninventive and uninspiring work of repairing the damage due to such flaws. It means attending to properties in things—their reparability—and capacities in individuals—their talents for mending—toward the atrophy of which there appear to be powerful economic incentives.

The story of *H. reparans* throws into sharp relief how we humans have responded to the fact of being creatures who are inherently limited by the resources at our disposal, who are subject to the ever present possibility of failure and decay, who sometimes seek continuity with the past, and who face the necessity of deciding whether or not to patch up relationships with our neighbors—in short, it reminds us of some facts about the human condition that perhaps we tend to find disturbing. And yet, once introduced, *Homo sapiens* as repairing animal typically invites gasps of recognition and suggestions that we've barely begun to explore the many projects and habitats of *H. reparans*.

NOTES

1. INTRODUCING *Homo reparans*

1. Pat Walsh, "Mr. Rhoades's Neighborhood," *Reader's Digest,* January 1995, 62–66.

2. See for example Robert Elliot, "Ecology and the Ethics of Environmental Restoration," in *Philosophy and the Natural Environment/Royal Institute of Philosophy Supplement: 36,* eds. Robin Attfield and Andrew Belsey (Cambridge, England: Cambridge University Press, 1994), 31–43.

3. "The Tool Man Cometh," *Ellsworth American,* June 27, 1997, 9–10.

4. Martha Minow, *Between Vengeance and Forgiveness: Facing History After Genocide and Mass Violence* (Boston: Beacon, 1998); Eric K. Yamamoto, *Interracial Justice: Conflict & Reconciliation in Post–Civil Rights America* (New York: NYU Press, 1999).

5. Jim Webb and Bart Houseman, with an introduction by Erma Bombeck (Garden City, N.J.: Doubleday, 1973).

6. Chris Black, "Where's Bill? Fiddling with His Legacy—and His Party," *The American Prospect,* February 25, 2002, 12.

7. Francis X. Clines, "A City Tries to Turn Candor into Consensus," *New York Times,* September 9, 2001, 16.

8. Carol Vogel, "Restored, but Still Blue," *New York Times,* January 4, 2002, B40.

9. *Consumer Reports,* cover titles August 2000, October 2001.

10. Hal Broom, Letters, *New York Times,* November 10, 2001.

11. Susan Dominus, "Mending a Psyche," and Lisa Belkin, "Life Without Father," *New York Times Magazine,* November 11, 2001, 69, 112.

12. Robert E. Rubin, "A Post-Disaster Economy in Need of Repair," *New York Times,* September 30, 2001, 13.

13. Andrew Pollack, "Digital Film Restoration Raises Questions About Fixing Flaws," *New York Times,* March 16, 1998, D1.

14. Katha Pollitt, "What's Right About Divorce," *New York Times,* June 27, 1997, A29.

15. Underfoot Floormat Company.

16. Dave Barry, "The Tool Man Cometh," *Ellsworth American,* June 27, 1997, 9.

17. Lawrence L. Langer, "The Alarmed Vision: Social Suffering and Holocaust Atrocity," *Daedalus,* vol. 125, no. 1 (winter 1996), 55.

18. Rose Macaulay, *Pleasure of Ruins* (New York: Walker and Company, 1966).

19. By Helene Liss, with the Loizeaux Family of Controlled Demolition, Inc. (New York: Black Dog and Leventhal Publishers, 2000).

20. Review of *Home Comforts: The Art and Science of Keeping House* (New York: Scribner, 2000) in *The New Yorker,* July 24, 2000, 75.

21. *Manchester Guardian Weekly,* September 15, 1996, 12.

2 . FROM BRICOLAGE TO INVISIBLE MENDING

1. Berkeley: University of California Press, 1987.

2. Harper, *Working Knowledge,* 126.

3. Fred Haefele, *Rebuilding the Indian. A Memoir* (New York: Riverhead Books, 1998), 9–10.

4. Elisabeth Bracht and Louise Wijnberg, *Bulletin Stedelijk Museum Amsterdam,* March 1998, 27–29.

5. Catherine Z. Elgin, "Restoration and Work Identity," chapter 5 of her *Between the Absolute and the Arbitrary* (Ithaca, N.Y.: Cornell University Press, 1997), 102.

6. Elgin here shows no particular interest in the social symbolism of patina, that which, for example, invites us "to read the duration of a family's status from the amount of the patina on it" (Grant McCracken, *Culture & Consumption: New Approaches to the Symbolic Character of Consumer Goods and Activities* [Bloomington: Indiana University Press, 1988], 36).

7. It surely is an open question whether Fred Haefele would have the same kind of passion for rebuilding his motorcycle were he to question the notion of authenticity along the lines of cultural critics such as Jean Beaudrillard, for whom such concern for the authentic involves an unexamined "obsession with certainty" (*The System of Objects* [London: Verso, 1996], 76); or Miles Orvell, who reads the "twentieth-century culture of authenticity" as an expression of "a functionalist ethos that sought to elevate the vernacular into the realm of high culture" (*The Real Thing: Imitation and Authenticity in American Culture, 1880–1940* [Chapel Hill: University of North Carolina Press, 1989], xvi).

3. THE HOUSEHOLD AS REPAIR SHOP

1. Catherine Hall, "The History of the Housewife," *The Politics of Housework,* ed. Ellen Malos (London: Allison & Busby, 1980), 49.

2. Edward Deming and Faith Andrews, *Work and Worship: The Economic Order of the Shakers* (Greenwich, Conn.: New York Graphic Society, 1974), 153–156, cited in Autumn Stanley, "Women Hold Up Two-Thirds of the Sky: Notes for a Revised History of Technology," in *Machina ex Dea: Feminist Perspectives on Technology,* ed. Joan Rothschild (New York: Pergamon Press, 1983), 9.

3. See Susan Eisenberg, *We'll Call You If We Need You: Experiences of Women Working Construction* (Ithaca: Cornell University Press, 1998), *passim.*

4. For example, *The New Practical Home Repair for Women: Your Questions Answered* by Bruce Cassiday (New York: Berkley Windhover, 1966, 1972); *The You-Don't Need-a-Man-to-Fix-It Book: The Woman's Guide to Confident Home Repair* by Jim Webb and Bart Houseman, with an introduction by Erma Bombeck (Garden City: Doubleday, 1973). A much more recent book alludes to earlier absence of women authors: *The Woman's Hands-on Home Repair Guide. Written by a Woman for Women* by Lyn Herrick (Pownal, Vt.: Storey Books, 1997).

5. Webb and Houseman, *You-Don't Need-a-Man-to-Fix-It Book,* 3. They also guess that "about four out of five men seem to be washouts as home repairers" (2).

6. Mary Baird, "Phone Repair Technician," in *Hard-Hatted Woman: Stories of Struggle and Success in the Trades,* ed. Molly Martin (Seattle: Seal Press, 1988), 249.

7. *Ibid.*

8. Steven Gelber, "Do-It-Yourself: Constructing, Repairing, and Maintaining Domestic Masculinity," in *The Gender and Consumer Culture Reader,* ed. Jennifer Scanlon (New York: New York University Press, 2000), 70–93.

9. *Ibid.,* 75.

10. See, for example, Dave Barry, "The Tool Man Cometh"; Phil McCombs, "Tooling Around Town," *Washington Post,* March 8, 1996, B5.

11. See Rent-a-Husband.com, described on its Web site as an organization "dedicated to meeting your needs as a homeowner, and enhancing the image of skilled craftsmen in the process."

12. *Frasier,* NBC, March 20, 2001. Is the brothers' contempt a defense against embarrassment over incompetence, or is their incompetence the intended fruit of their contempt?

13. Bruce Cassiday, *New Practical Home Repair for Women,* 1; Una Robertson, *The Illustrated History of the Housewife, 1650–1950* (New York: St. Martin's, 1997), 152–153.

14. This happened first among the urban middle classes, but eventually reached rural and working-class populations as well. See Tamara K. Hareven, "The Home and the Family in Historical Perspective," in *Home: A Place in the World,* ed. Arien Mack (New York: New York University Press, 1993), 246ff.

15. Christopher Lasch, *Haven in a Heartless World: The Family Besieged* (New York: Basic Books, 1979).

16. See, for example, Carol Stack, *All Our Kin: Strategies for Survival in a Black Community* (New York: Harper & Row, 1974); Eleanor Leacock, "Postscript: Implications for Organization," in *Women's Work: Development and the Division of Labor by Gender,* eds. Eleanor Leacock and Helen I. Safa (South Hadley, Mass.: Bergin & Garvey, 1986), 253–265.

17. Judith Martin, *Miss Manners' Guide to Domestic Tranquility: The Authoritative Manual for Every Civilized Household, However Harried* (New York: Three Rivers Press, 1999), 2.

18. Stephanie Nano, "Doctors Find a Hint Hearts Can Self-Repair," *Boston Globe,* January 3, 2002, A2.

19. See descriptions of healing practices in, for example, *Coyote Medicine* by Lewis Mehl-Madrona (New York: Scribner, 1997); Gay Wilentz, *Healing Narratives: Women Writers Curing Cultural Disease* (New Brunswick, N.J.: Rutgers University Press, 2000).

20. Describing the ongoing work of 1920s British working-class women even in the last stages of pregnancy, Marjorie Spring Rice pointed out, "Even if she is in bed, she . . . can direct operations, even perhaps doing some of the 'smaller' jobs herself—like drying crockery, ironing, and of course the eternal mending." From "Working Class Wives," in *The Politics of Housework,* ed. Ellen Malos (London: Allison & Busby, 1980), 92.

21. Melanie Klein, "Love, Guilt and Reparation," in *Love, Hate and Reparation,* by Melanie Klein and Joan Riviere (New York: Norton, 1964), 61. The sense that reparation is successful may be hard to achieve: "The desire to control the object, the sadistic gratification of overcoming and humiliating it, of getting the better of it, the *triumph* over it, may enter so strongly into the act of reparation (carried out by thoughts, activities or sublima-

tions) that the benign circle started by this act becomes broken. The objects which were to be restored change again into persecutors, and in turn paranoid fears are revived." Klein, "Mourning and Its Relation to Manic-Depressive States," in *The Selected Melanie Klein*, ed. Juliet Mitchell (New York: Free Press, 1986), 153.

22. Sally Greene explores such a theme in the stories of Elizabeth Spencer. "Mending Webs: The Challenge of Childhood in Elizabeth Spencer's Short Fiction," *Mississippi Quarterly*, vol. 49, no. 1 (1996), 89–98.

23. Arlie Russell Hochschild, *Time Bind: When Work Becomes Home and Home Becomes Work* (New York: Henry Holt, 1997), 209–210.

24. Guy Gugliotta, " 'Self-Healing' Plastic Reported," *Boston Globe,* February 15, 2001, A7. "Using high-tech materials and a low-tech concept inspired by the human body, the scientists devised a process that can continuously repair and regenerate the chemical soup that makes up most plastics by activating special resin-filled capsules stored within the material itself."

25. Katie Geneva Cannon, essay in *Hard Times Cotton Mill Girls: Personal Histories of Womanhood and Poverty in the South,* ed. Victoria Byerly (Ithaca, N.Y.: ILR Press, 1986), 36.

26. *Ibid.*

27. See Judith Rollins, *Between Women: Domestics and Their Employers* (Philadelphia: Temple University Press, 1985).

28. Cannon, in *Hard Times Cotton Mill Girls,* 38–39.

29. The notion of the toxic workplace is highlighted in Barbara Reinhold's *Toxic Work: How to Overcome Stress, Overload, and Burnout and Revitalize Your Career* (New York: Penguin Plume, 1997).

30. Linda Marvin, *Housekeeping Made Easy: More than 2,000 Shortcuts for Daily Household Living* (New York: Vanguard, 1943), 237.

31. Gelber, "Do-It-Yourself," 73.

32. See, for example, Harriet Jacobs, *Incidents in the Life of a Slave Girl, Written by Herself* [1861], ed. Jean Fagan Yellin (Cambridge, Mass.: Harvard University Press, 1987).

33. Una Robertson's (*Illustrated History of the Housewife,* 150) recitation of the daily or weekly tasks of the English housewife until surprisingly recently is not atypical: "cooking, cleaning, fetching water and fuel, making candles, washing and ironing, producing food from the garden, looking after poultry, pigs, or bees, going to market to sell products of her own making or to buy in what was required, supervising servants [many of them also females of the household], caring for children and other dependents." My inquiry into the kinds of repair women do in the household is meant to complement such a list.

34. See, for example, Katie Cannon, in *Hard Times Cotton Mill Girls;* Jacqueline Jones, *Labor of Love, Labor of Sorrow: Black Women, Work and the Family, from Slavery to the Present* (New York: Random House, 1986), 4.

35. Daniel Robb, author of *Crossing the Water: Eighteen Months on an Island Working with Troubled Boys* (New York: Simon & Schuster, 2001). Comment heard on *Talk of the Nation* (National Public Radio), May 30, 2001.

36. The metaphor of a moral compass is a bit misleading, since there is no debate about the possibility of more than one "true north," while there are ongoing debates about whether there might be equally valid moral laws pointing in conflicting directions.

37. For sustained discussion, see Robin West, *Caring for Justice* (New York: New York University Press, 1997); Joan Tronto, *Moral Boundaries: A Political Argument for an Ethic of Care* (New York: Routledge, 1993).

38. See, for example, Barbara Houston, "Prolegomena to Future Caring," in *A Reader in Feminist Ethics,* ed. Debra Shogan (Toronto: Canadian Scholars Press, 1992), 109–127.

39. See for example Judith Rollins, *Between Women;* Katie Cannon, in *Hard Times Cotton Mill Girls;* Harriet Jacobs, *Incidents in the Life of a Slave Girl.*

40. Houston, "Prolegomena," 113.

41. Editors' introduction, *Women and Moral Theory,* eds. Eva Feder Kittay and Diana T. Meyers (Totowa, N.J.: Rowman & Littlefield, 1987), 3.

42. Cheshire Calhoun, "Emotional Work," in *Explorations in Feminist Ethics: Theory and Practice,* eds. Eve Browning Cole and Susan Coultrap-McQuin (Bloomington: Indiana University Press, 1992), 118.

4. SERVING TIME IN THE COMMUNITY OF REPAIRERS

1. David Lerman, "Restoring Justice," *Tikkun,* September/October 1999, 13.

2. Promotion of National Unity and Reconciliation Act, No. 34 of 1995, in 1 1995 JSRSA 2–385, Preamble P1. Quoted in Marianne Guela, "Note: South Africa's Truth and Reconciliation Commission as an Alternate Means of Addressing Transitional Government Conflicts in a Divided Society," *Boston University International Law Journal,* vol. 18 (spring 2000), 64.

3. Leena Kurki, "Restorative and Community Justice in the United States," *Crime and Justice,* vol. 27 (2000), 237.

4. This, of course, presupposes a host of institutions and people: "The people inside the system of criminal justice include, among others, the experts who draft the criminal codes and tinker with the language, and the legislatures that make the codes into laws," and also "police, detectives, narcotics agents, judges, juries grand and small, prosecutors and defenders, prison guards and wardens, probation officers, parole board members." Lawrence Friedman, *Crime and Punishment in American History* (New York: Basic Books, 1993), 5.

5. Lawrence Friedman reminds us that in the nineteenth century there were attempts to distinguish salvageable from unsalvageable convicts, the "incorrigibles" from the "savable ones," but by the late twentieth century, "rightly or wrongly, hardly anyone believes [that prison might rehabilitate prisoners] anymore." Lawrence Friedman, *American Law: An Introduction* (New York: Norton, 1984), 171, 172. See also Marc Mauer, who in *The Race to Incarcerate* (New York: New Press, 1999) describes worries from the left about the coercive possibilities inherent in rehabilitation and doubts from the right about the success rates of rehabilitation but also

about its appropriateness as a response to crime. See also Joseph T. Halli-nan, *Going Up the River: Travels in a Prison Nation* (New York: Random House, 2001).

6. Lerman, "Restoring Justice," 13.

7. David Cole, *No Equal Justice: Race and Class in the American Criminal Jus-tice System* (New York: New Press, 1999), 196.

8. See, for example, Ann Arnett Ferguson, *Bad Boys: Public Schools in the Making of Black Masculinity* (Ann Arbor: University of Michigan Press, 2000), on presumptions about young black males as "incorrigible, irre-mediable, unsalvageable" (90).

9. Frederick W. Gay, "Restorative Justice and the Prosecutor," *Fordham Urban Law Journal,* vol. 27 (June 2000), 1652.

10. Bob Herbert, "The Fatal Flaw," *New York Times,* February 11, 2002.

11. See, for example, Friedman, *American Law,* 174.

12. It is well known that the TRC has hardly been universally embraced by apartheid's victims. For a review of the TRC's strengths and weak-nesses by a legal scholar who himself writes in a framework of repair, see Eric Yamamoto, "Race Apologies," *Journal of Gender, Race and Justice,* vol. 1, no. 1 (1997), 47–88.

13. Tina Rosenberg, "Truth Commissions Take on a Local Flavor," *New York Times,* February 26, 2001, A18.

14. Lerman, "Restoring Justice," 14.

15. "Discussion Paper: From Restorative Justice to Transformative Jus-tice," Law Commission of Canada, Catalogue no. JL2–6/1999, 28.

16. *Ibid.,* 11.

17. Guela, "South Africa's Truth and Reconciliation Commission," 74.

18. See, for example, Robert Yazzie, "Life Comes from It: Navajo Justice Concepts," *New Mexico Law Review,* vol. 24 (1994), 175ff.; Laurie A. Arsenault, "The Great Excavation: 'Discovering' Navajo Tribal Peace-making within the Anglo-American Family System," *Ohio State Journal on Dispute Resolution,* vol. 15 (2000), 795–823.

19. Jennifer J. Llewellyn and Robert Howse, "Restorative Justice—A Conceptual Framework," unpublished manuscript prepared for the Law Commission of Canada, 15.

20. Howard Zehr, *Changing Lenses: A New Focus for Crime and Justice* (Waterloo, Ontario: Herald Press, 1990), 100, quoted in Llewellyn and Howse, "Restorative Justice," 7. This echoes the discussion of an "ethics of care" and "ethics of justice" in chapter 3.

21. Llewellyn and Howse, "Restorative Justice," 4, quoting John Braithwaite.

22. Danielle S. Allen, "Democratic Dis-ease: Of Anger and the Troubling Nature of Punishment," in *The Passions of Law,* ed. Susan A. Bandes (New York: New York University Press, 1999), 191–214.

23. Llewellyn and Howse, "Restorative Justice," 8.

24. Lerman, "Restoring Justice," 15.

25. Richard Delgado, "Goodbye to Hammurabi: Analyzing the Atavistic Appeal of Restorative Justice," *Stanford Law Review,* vol. 52, no. 4 (April 2000), 757.

26. Kurki, "Restorative and Community Justice," 268.

27. Arsenault, "The Great Excavation," 797–798.

28. Harper, *Working Knowledge,* 169.

29. See, for example, Richard Delgado, "Goodbye to Hammurabi," 765: "Mediation treats the *victim* respectfully, according him the status of an end-in-himself, while the offender is treated as a thing to be managed, shamed, and conditioned."

30. Delgado, "Goodbye to Hammurabi," 770–771.

31. Amy Gutmann and Dennis Thompson, "The Moral Foundations of Truth Commissions," in *Truth v. Justice,* eds. Robert I. Rotberg and Dennis Thompson (Princeton, N.J.: Princeton University Press, 2000), 32–33.

5. IN THE TOOLBOX: WORDS AND MONEY

1. See Boris Bittker, *The Case for Black Reparations* (New York: Random House, 1973).

2. *The Debt: What America Owes to Blacks* (New York: Dutton, 2000).

3. See, for example, Manning Marable, *How Capitalism Underdeveloped Black America,* updated edition (Cambridge, Mass.: South End Press, 2000); Dalton Conley, *Being Black, Living in the Red: Race, Wealth, and Social Policy in America* (Berkeley: University of California Press, 1999).

4. Indeed, recent developments in tort law have been criticized for commodifying pain and love. See, for example, Richard Abel's essay "Torts" in *The Politics of Law: A Progressive Critique,* rev. ed., ed. David Kairys (New York: Pantheon, 1990), 326–349.

5. See, for example, William Glaberson, "Lawyers' Math in Sept. 11 Deaths Shows Varying Values for Life," *New York Times,* November 11, 2001, B1; Ellen Goodman, "Putting a Price Tag on Life," *Boston Globe,* January 6, 2002, E7.

6. "When we resort to excuse, explanation, or justification, we necessarily attempt to distance ourselves from our actions and our unique personal identities. We deny or suspend the imperatives of responsibility and answerability. We appeal, variously, to an impaired self, for example, diminished capacity or external forces (coercion, accident, or even, on occasion, the miraculous) to exonerate our doings and their consequences." Nicholas Tavuchis, *Mea Culpa: A Sociology of Apology and Reconciliation* (Stanford, Calif.: Stanford University Press, 1991), 19.

7. Tavuchis, *Mea Culpa,* 13 and passim.

8. Jean Améry, *At the Mind's Limits: Contemplations by a Survivor of Auschwitz and Its Realities* (New York: Schocken Books, 1986), 62–81.

9. Alison Mitchell, "Survivors of Tuskegee Study Get Apology from Clinton," *New York Times,* May 17, 1997, 10.

10. For one thing, the more participants in and witnesses to an apology, the more of a performance it becomes, which in turn invites questions about its sincerity.

11. *The Fire Next Time* (New York: Dell, 1963), 15.

12. Baldwin, *The Price of the Ticket* (New York: St. Martin's, 1985), 536.

13. The point here is not unlike that the writer Verlyn Klinkenborg made in reference to 1960s California: "Its sins [were] undone by the frankness with which they were revealed." *New York Times,* January 29, 2001, A26.

14. Tavuchis, *Mea Culpa,* 18.

15. Baldwin, *Fire Next Time,* 16.

16. The term is borrowed from Martin Pernick, *A Calculus of Suffering: Pain, Professionalism, and Anesthesia in Nineteenth-Century America* (New York: Columbia University Press, 1985).

6. THE IRREPARABLE AND THE IRREDEEMABLE

1. Georg Simmel, "The Ruin," in *Essays on Sociology, Philosophy and Aesthetics,* ed. Kurt H. Wolff (New York: Harper & Row, 1965), 259–266. Quoted in *Irresistible Decay: Ruins Reclaimed,* by Michael S. Roth with Claire Lyons and Charles Merewether (Los Angeles: Getty Research Institute for the History of Art and the Humanities, 1997).

2. Anne F. Janowitz, *England's Ruins: Poetic Purpose and the National Landscape* (Cambridge, Mass.: Blackwell, 1990), 37, quoting John Dyer.

3. Rose Macaulay, *Pleasure of Ruins,* 40.

4. *Ibid.,* 255.

5. *Ibid.,* 76.

6. *Ibid.,* xv–xvi.

7. Paul Zucker, *Fascination of Decay. Ruins: Relic-Symbol-Ornament* (Ridgewood, N.J.: Gregg Press, 1968); Roth, Lyons, and Merewether, *Irresistible Decay.*

8. Robert Harbison, *The Built, the Unbuilt and the Unbuildable: In Pursuit of Architectural Meaning* (Cambridge, Mass.: MIT Press, 1991), 108.

9. Michael Roth, "Irresistible Decay: Ruins Reclaimed," in Roth, Lyons, and Merewether, *Irresistible Decay,* 5.

10. Macaulay, *Pleasure of Ruins,* 99.

11. *Ibid.,* 12.

12. Roth, "Irresistible Decay," 1.

13. Zucker, *Fascination of Decay,* 161.

14. *Ibid.,* 37.

15. Macaulay, *Pleasure of Ruins,* 301.

16. *Ibid.,* 261.

17. Roth, "Irresistible Decay," 18.

18. Macaulay, *Pleasure of Ruins,* 18, quoting John Earle, *Microcosmographie* (1628).

19. Quoted by Reg Saner, *Reaching Keet Seel: Ruin's Echo and the Anasazi* (Salt Lake City: University of Utah Press, 1998), 86.

20. A National Park Service account of the history of its ruins stabilization projects boasts of its efforts to support the peoples whose lands it controls: the "mobile ruins stabilization units," which moved from one Southwestern site to another, included two generations of Navajos, about whom we are supposed to be relieved to learn: "Native patience, artisanship, and resourcefulness, coupled with adaptation to isolated locations under camp conditions, have earned for the Navajo first choice as members of specialized field crews." *Ruins Stabilization in the Southwestern United States,* compiled by Roland Von S. Richert and R. Gordon Vivian (Washington, D.C.: National Park Service, U.S. Department of the Interior, 1974), 2.

21. Roth, "Irresistible Decay," 7.

22. *Ibid.,* 15.

23. Rose Macaulay, *Non-Combatants and Others* (London: Methuen, 1986 [1916]).

24. Roth, "Irresistible Decay," 8.

25. Macaulay, *Pleasure of Ruins,* 56, 279.

26. Herbert Muschamp, "The Commemorative Beauty of Tragic Wreckage," *New York Times,* Arts and Leisure, November 11, 2001, 37.

27. Dolores Hayden, *The Power of Place: Urban Landscapes as Public History* (Cambridge, Mass.: MIT Press, 1997), 6.

28. Harbison, *Built, the Unbuilt and the Unbuildable,* 121ff. Indeed, "Old ruins only *look* doomed anymore, these plants and factories *are.*"

29. But this distinction itself is at question in Camilo Jose Vergara's photographs of abandoned buildings and lots in cities such as Detroit and Camden: "In contrast to those who see these ruins as failures and eyesores, that are best forgotten, I record urban decay with a combined sense of respect, loss, and admiration for its peculiar beauty." *American Ruins* (New York: Monacelli Press, 1999), 11.

30. *Holocaust Testimonies: The Ruins of Memory* (New Haven, Conn.: Yale University Press, 1991).

31. *Pre-empting the Holocaust* (New Haven, Conn.: Yale University Press, 1998).

32. Langer also finds evidence of the logic of redemption and salvation in some of the *written* testimonies of survivors, the message of which is belied by the less guarded, less narratively structured and guided accounts that they give orally. Of Jean Améry, for example, he says, "His writing constitutes the reconciliation or the integration whose success oral testimony dramatically disputes" (*Holocaust Testimonies,* 91).

33. Langer, *Holocaust Testimonies,* 136 (quoting survivor identified as Julia S.).

34. *Ibid.,* 144.

35. *Ibid.,* 92.

36. *Ibid.,* 83–84, 140, 146, 189.

37. Langer, *Pre-empting the Holocaust,* xv.

38. Lebbeus Woods, *Radical Reconstruction* (New York: Princeton Architectural Press, 1997). "Wherever buildings are broken by the explosion of

bombs or artillery shells, by lack of maintenance or repair, by fire or structural collapse, their form must be respected in its integrity, embodying a history that must not be denied" (15).

39. Langer, *Holocaust Testimonies,* 38.

40. Langer, *Pre-empting the Holocaust,* 72.

41. Langer, *Holocaust Testimonies,* 68–69.

42. *Ibid.,* 43–44.

43. Langer, *Pre-empting the Holocaust,* 78.

44. *Ibid.,* xvii.

45. Langer, *Holocaust Testimonies,* 50, 79, 146.

46. Langer, *Pre-empting the Holocaust,* 68.

47. *Ibid.,* 88.

48. Langer's wariness about the use of the word *reconciliation* extends to a concern that pursuing reconciliation rather than justice [see chapter 4] in places such as South Africa, Argentina, and so forth "may create a fragile peace in communities wearied by seemingly endless periods of anguish," but he thinks that it involves a failure to come to grips with atrocity: "Such avoidance resembles the attitude of those who use the texts of the Holocaust testimonies as examples of 'working through' past traumas toward a goal of reconciled understanding and a liberating growth into the future" though in fact the testimonies "reflect hundreds of instances of unredeemed and unredeemable loss" (*Pre-empting the Holocaust,* 67). There is no reason to think that Langer's views necessarily vitiate monetary reparations and other forms of compensation from the German, Austrian, and Swiss governments, since what concerns him is the redemptive logic of salvation and reconciliation, not attempts to return property or make up for unpaid labor and financial losses.

49. Fox Butterfield, "Inmate Rehabilitation Returns as Prison Goal," *New York Times,* May 20, 2001, 1, 26.

50. "Facts About Prisons and Prisoners," from Bureau of Justice Statistics and The Sentencing Project <www.sentencingproject.org/brief/pub1035.pdf>. Visited January 12, 2002. See also Marc Mauer, *Race to In-*

carcerate, 118–141; Angela Y. Davis and Cassandra Shaylor, "Race, Gender, and the Prison Industrial Complex: California and Beyond," *Meridians,* vol. 2, no. 1 (2001): 1–25.

7. REPAIR, THE OLD, AND THE NEW

1. James Marston Fitch, *Historic Preservation: Curatorial Management of the Built World* (Charlottesville: University Press of Virginia, 1990), 46.

2. *Art and Technics* (New York: Columbia University Press, 1952), 42.

3. Jane Perlez, "Decay of a 20th Century Relic: What's the Future of Auschwitz?" *New York Times,* January 5, 1994, A6.

4. Harper, *Working Knowledge,* 127.

5. Sander Gilman, *Making the Body Beautiful: A Cultural History of Aesthetic Surgery* (Princeton, N.J.: Princeton University Press, 1999), 45.

6. Michael Paulson, "Morality Meets Biology in Gene Project," *Boston Globe,* July 10, 2000, A5.

7. Harper, *Working Knowledge,* 34.

8. *Ibid.,* 169.

9. Conversation with Bob Abrams, owner of Gateway Motors in Northampton, Mass.

10. Edward Mendelson, "Revision and Power: The Example of W. H. Auden," *YFS* [Yale French Studies], no. 89, *Drafts,* ed. Michel Contat, Denis Hollier, Jacques Neefs, and Alyson Waters (1996), 112.

11. See, for example, *A Piece of Work: Five Writers Discuss Their Revisions,* ed. Jay Woodruff (Iowa City: University of Iowa Press, 1993); Liz Lerman, "Toward a Process for Critical Response," in her *Are Miracles Enough? Selected Writings on Art and Community 1983–1994* (Takoma Park, Md.: Dance Exchange, 1995), 17–19; Valerie Miner, "To Look Again: An Essay on Revision," *AWP Chronicle,* February 1998, 31–34.

12. Harper, *Working Knowledge,* 5.

13. Thanks to Bill Streeter, owner of the Silver Maple Bindery in Northampton, Mass., for this and many other rich examples.

14. Fitch, *Historic Preservation*.

15. Among prominent recent explorers of creativity is Mihaly Csikszent-mihalyi. See, for example, his *Creativity: Flow and the Psychology of Discovery and Invention* (New York: HarperCollinsPublishers, 1996).

16. Glenn Collins, "When G.I. Joe Calls Out for a Medic," *New York Times,* February 11, 2001, 33.

ACKNOWLEDGMENTS

Not all the flaws in this book will have been fixed by the time it goes to press, but that's hardly the fault of the posse of repairers who so generously aided and abetted me in this project.

The First Year Seminar program at Smith College made it possible for me to benefit from sustained discussions with students enrolled at various times in FYS 112, The Work of Repair: Vanessa Bombardieri, Meghan Crutchley, Erika Deraleau, Kathryn Finley, Rachel Hackett, Lauren Lessard, and Carrie Mowbray; Alya Al-Saud, Abigail Allen, Amy Doucha, Kim Fenol, Christina Forrestal, Jennifer Frederick, Annette Georgia, Jessica Gregorie, Michaela Kelly, Sarai King, Gina Lappano, Jumana Madanat, Melina Packer, Carissa Smith, Courtney Sullivan, Nora Wilkins, and Amalia Zagorski; Jessica Arista, Ceilidh Auger-Day, Christine Basta, Brooke Betts, Chelsea Brown, Brianna Dieter, Megan Ferguson, Alexandra Fischer, Fopefolu Folowosele, Hope Freeman, Rebecca

Gordon, Victoria Green, Lauren Kemp, Bayley Kersbergen, Katherine McCarthy, Zoe Meyer, Yashira Pepin, Sarah Rogers, and Emily Royce. Lindsay Lawyer, Nicole Mailman, and Laura Passin, ingenious repair researchers, made sure my files were always overflowing with annotated references to books, articles, films, and Web sites.

Not the least of the pleasures of this project has been the high spirit with which friends, colleagues and family members have gone out of their way to ply me with examples of repair from every nook and cranny of the human landscape: Ann Arnett Ferguson, Frances Smith Foster, Andrea Hairston, Betsey Harries, Alice Hearst, Annie Jones, Ann Leone, Helen Longino, Dorothy Smith Patterson, Kevin Quashie, Molly Shanley, Ruth Solie, Jon Spelman, Jenn Whiting, Deborah Wolf. Among the most satisfying parts of this investigation has been listening to repairers from various fields reflect on the nature of their work: Bob Abrams, Martin Born, Howard Ewert, Linda Fidnick, Scott Girard, Donna Gunn, John Hoogstraten, David Lerman, Liz Lerman, Avery Rimer, Judy Scales-Trent, Scott Schmidt, Bill Streeter, Tom the Piano Restorer, Louise Wijnberg, Eric Yamamoto.

For their incisive questions and fruitful suggestions, I'm grateful to audiences at Southern Connecticut State College, the University of New Hampshire, Binghamton University, the University of Alberta at Edmonton, the University of California at Los Angeles, the University of San Francisco, Greenfield Community College, the University of Memphis Law School, Washington State University at Pullman, and Smith College. Warm thanks to

Amy Macdonald and Christopher Lydon for the invitation a few years ago to talk about this project on "The Connection" (from WBUR-Boston) and chat over the airwaves with repair mavens up and down the East Coast.

For their close and careful readings of all or part of the manuscript, I remain happily and gratefully indebted to Kum-Kum Bhavnani, Nalini Bhushan, Sue Campbell, Martha Minow, Al Mosley, Joe Singer, Cornelia Spelman, Peter Stallybrass, Geri Thoma. I marvel at and rejoice in such deep acts of friendship and collegiality.

Andy Hrycyna helped clarify some of my earliest ideas about this project some years ago, even as he was getting to press an earlier book of mine with Beacon. Deb Chasman's unmistakable enthusiasm for the manuscript was just the right gift at just the right time. Working with Julie Hassel, the editorial shepherd of *Repair,* has been an unmitigated delight.

INDEX